DRILL TO SKILL

TEACHER TACTICS IN PHYSICAL EDUCATION

DRILL TO SKILL

TEACHER TACTICS IN PHYSICAL EDUCATION

CONNIE BLAKEMORE
Brigham Young University

NENA HAWKES
Brigham Young University

EVELYN BURTON
Alpine School District - Aspen Elementary School

WCB Wm. C. Brown Publishers

Cover design by Jeanne Marie Regan

Illustrations by John B. Burton

Copyright © 1991 by Wm. C. Brown Publishers. All rights reserved

Library of Congress Catalog Card Number: 89–62743

ISBN 0–697–04457–2

Printed in the United States of America by Wm. C. Brown Publishers,
2460 Kerper Boulevard, Dubuque, IA 52001

10 9 8 7 6 5 4 3 2 1

CONTENTS

PREFACE

DRILL TO SKILL is a book of teacher tactics purposely designed for those who teach a variety of sport activities. It is unique and functional because drills for many sports and activities are under one cover giving practitioners a handbook that is easily understood and applied. The instructional ideas found in the text will aid physical education teachers K–12 to: 1) provide practice content for improving skill performance, 2) provide the transition from drill to game situations, 3) formally evaluate performance, and 4) provide motivation and enjoyment. This book is focused on sports that are most often taught by teachers in middle, junior, and senior high schools. The text begins with an introductory chapter to discuss the organizational considerations necessary to conduct a successful physical education class. Each of eight chapters include popular sports with a concluding multiapplication chapter.

Each chapter is formulated to assist the teacher. Specific aids include: 1) equipment needed, 2) suggestions for instructional proficiency, 3) teaching progressions, 4) drills, from simple to complex, 5) lead-up games, 6) skill tests, and 7) written exam questions. Directions are written in a simple step-by-step approach, accompanied by illustrations that clarify each activity.

The book is designed to help students in training and professionals in practice. It does not attempt to present or analyze skill. Rather, the goal has been to present teacher tactics based on sound field-tested principles obtained from professionals who have taught, coached, and participated at every level of education.

ACKNOWLEDGMENTS

We dedicate this book to our students, past and present. They have filled our days with excitement, laughter, and a sense of accomplishment.

A special note of appreciation is extended to John B. Burton who illustrated the book with his heart and his hands. His gentle, kind ways grace all of his endeavors.

CHAPTER ONE

PLANNING FOR SUCCESSFUL TEACHING

"THOSE WHO FAIL TO PLAN, PLAN TO FAIL"

The effective teacher creates a learning environment that reflects energy and enthusiasm. These teacher-generated qualities are then reflected by students as they participate.

Students will not express themselves in a snappy, vigorous manner unless the teacher first portrays these qualities. An indecisive, uncertain teacher most often creates an atmosphere that smothers the students' energy.

Although the teacher's own personal qualities and attitudes greatly affect student behavior and class atmosphere, the underlying strength of the exceptional teacher is *preparation.* Nothing, absolutely nothing, can substitute for thorough preparation. Effective teachers are confident, assured, and poised because they preplan completely and invest time mastering their subject matter.

STUDENT GOALS AND OBJECTIVES

To enhance planning and achieve results, the teacher should determine both general long-term goals and specific short-term objectives. For example, a fitness goal might be that "each student will improve one fitness category in the AAHPERD Physical Best tests." A short-term objective for this fitness goal might be that "students will perform aerobic conditioning activities for fifteen minutes during class, three times per week."

The teacher should define the goals for the year before teaching begins. The objectives for each unit must be designed to achieve the long-term goals. To determine whether goals will be met, it is necessary to evaluate the objectives on a regular basis.

EVALUATION OF STUDENTS

Evaluation is the means used to determine student performance. Evaluation takes two forms. First, **preassessment** helps determine the current skill levels of students prior to instruction. Once the preassessment information has been gathered, the teacher must design learning experiences to meet the needs of all students. The second form of evaluation is accomplished during the instructional unit. It may be either **formative** (continuous throughout the unit) or **summative** (concluding a unit).

Preassessment

Preassessment occurs before teaching begins. The elementary teacher is primarily concerned with preassessing locomotor movements such as hopping, skipping, running, galloping, jumping, and sliding; and basic skills such as throwing, catching, striking, and kicking. These skills and movement patterns are basic to all psychomotor performance.

The secondary teacher preassesses student skill performance to finalize unit plans. For example, when basketball is the instructional activity, testing might measure dribbling, passing, and shooting skills. Instructional plans should then build on and elevate present levels of student performance.

Formative and Summative Testing

Formative testing is continuous and systematic throughout a unit of instruction. On the other hand, summative testing is comprehensive and is conducted at the conclusion of a unit. These evaluation tools may include skill tests, written exams, tournament results, and teacher ratings or checklists. All classroom instruction should include such measurement devices to monitor student progress and achievement.

Evaluation implies that a teacher has not left instruction to chance. "Throw out the ball" procedures that omit teaching and testing are, in fact, "throw out the program" tactics.

Skill Development

Practice, a critical part of skill acquisition and improvement, must include numerous repetitions of correct practice patterns, or skill development is seriously hampered. Unfortunately, skill practice often perfects an incorrect skill. A two-step solution to this problem would be to (1) teach beginners correctly by identifying and correcting errors early in the learning process, well before the skill is grooved; and (2) produce and practice drills that are as gamelike as possible.

The second practice step, producing and practicing gamelike drills, is the focus of this text. Certain fundamentals are essential to drill development and use. Without an understanding of these fundamentals, instructors often teach drills nonsequentially, thus confusing the learner and frustrating the development of progressive skills.

GETTING READY FOR INSTRUCTION

Certain preliminary steps should be followed in preparation for class instruction. Students must be oriented to the facilities and the system of operation. Each student will probably need a locker (perhaps a lock) and a gym suit before the first class. Teachers must provide complete information about these items before instruction can begin.

Orientation

Students need to know class operational procedures from the first day of class. (Hints for establishing such policies are contained throughout this chapter.)

New students will benefit from a tour of the locker room and showers, equipment room, pool, gymnasium, gymnastics area, dance studio, weight room, and outside playing areas. Teachers might want to point out safety procedures and special rules regarding the care and upkeep of each facility along the way.

Lockers

Accurate lock and locker records should be kept and stored in a place unavailable to students. Each record must include student name, locker number, and lock combination. When students are required to furnish their own locks, a combination lock is recommended.

Assign lockers evenly throughout the locker room for each class. For example, the locker room may include four sections with lockers stacked in five rows. In this case, the first-period class would be assigned evenly to each of the four sections on row number one. Period two would be assigned evenly to each of the four sections on row number two. Continue in this fashion for all class periods. This arrangement reduces overcrowding in any one section of the locker room.

The Dress Policy

Some schools require each student to wear a standard, regulation uniform. Teachers should describe this uniform to students and provide information pertaining to its purchase. Even in schools that do not require a regulation uniform, teachers should establish a reasonable dress policy. Students should wear gym shoes and stockings for all activities, other than specialized classes such as dance and gymnastics, to prevent accidents and possible litigation. Discourage students from wearing clothing that inhibits movement or is distracting. Keep in mind that the "I don't care what you wear" policy often promotes a lack of respect and contributes to poor class control and unsafe conditions.

The following commonly asked student questions are listed for consideration and thought. Answers to these questions will establish an important part of the dress policy.

1. "Can I wear these shoes? They have rubber soles." (or black soles, crepe soles, or cleats)
2. "Are cutoffs OK?"
3. "Can I wear my spandex under my shorts?"
4. "Can I wear the clothes I have on?"
5. "Do I have to take off my nylons?"
6. "Can I wear 'sweats'?"

7. "Why do I need to bring a clean suit every week? I don't sweat."
8. "Can I go without socks?"
9. "Somebody took my gym clothes. Can I still play?"

Motivated, enthusiastic students want to be part of the action. They will usually dress for participation if the class provides a successful and enjoyable experience. Students who do not dress for participation, and yet are allowed to remain in the activity area, often distract other students and disturb class activity. An unattractive alternative to not dressing usually encourages students to dress and participate. Students who come to class unable to participate because of illness, injury, or other extenuating circumstances may act as scorekeepers, linesmen, or timers in a drill or game.

ORGANIZE THE CLASS

Class organization often determines the difference between a good teacher and an excellent teacher. Helpful hints follow to assist the teacher in organizing and motivating students.

Grade Policy

Grades should reflect student participation and achievement in the physical education class. Grading is an issue that creates philosophical differences. Some teachers feel that the student who comes regularly, complies with class polices, and performs with maximum effort should receive an "A," or outstanding grade. Others argue that the student should only receive an "A" when actual performance is superior. Whichever position individual teachers take, they must establish measurable criteria to evaluate student performance. These criteria should be clearly defined and explained to students at the beginning of each course or unit.

Guidelines
The following guidelines should be considered when developing grading policies:

1. Develop a grading structure that includes specific components such as skill, knowledge, and participation.
2. Include evaluation procedures that accurately measure each grading component such as skill tests, written tests, and checklists. It is difficult to measure how hard a student "tries" or whether the student is a "good sport." If teachers use effort and attitude as grade components, they must explain to students how these qualities are defined and appraised.
3. Provide opportunities for all students to succeed. Focus on each student by individualizing practice techniques, allowing make-up work within time limits, and selecting the best test result from multiple scores. Never base a grade entirely on the outcome of one skill test.

Students will want specific details regarding grading policies. The following common student questions are presented for consideration:

1. "What percentage of my grade depends on skill test results?"
2. "If 40 percent of my grade is based on participation, what exactly must I do to participate?"
3. "Is there any way I can earn bonus points or extra credit?"
4. "How many times can I 'cut' class before my grade is lowered?"
5. "What is the penalty for being late to class?"
6. "Will an excused absence affect my grade?"
7. "How can I prove to you that I'm doing my best?"
8. "If I come every day, will I get an 'A' for effort?"
9. "Do you throw out the lowest test score?"
10. "What if my team never wins? Will it affect my grade?"
11. "If I have the highest score on a skill test, will that assure me of an 'A'?"

Sample Grading Policy (Basketball)

Skill (50 percent).   Formative tests will be given throughout the unit. The best score will be recorded the final day of testing or whenever the student is satisfied with the grade.

Timed Dribble	**Free Shots**	**Thirty-Second Shoot**
A = 11 seconds	A = 4 out of 5	A = 15 shots
B = 12 seconds	B = 3 out of 5	B = 13 shots
C = 15 seconds	C = 2 out of 5	C = 9 shots
D = 16 seconds	D = 1 out of 5	D = 7 shots

GAME PLAY EXECUTION (CHECKLIST)

DRIBBLING	**EXECUTION**
Eyes up	__ __ __ __
Ball waist high or lower	__ __ __ __
Nondribbling hand up for protection	__ __ __ __

A = All areas executed
B = One area needs improvement
C = Two areas need improvement
D = Three areas need improvement

Written Test (25 percent)
A = 90 percent or higher
B = 70–89 percent
C = 45–69 percent
D = 25–44 percent

Participation (15 percent)
A = 0 unexcused absences
B = One unexcused absence
C = Two or three unexcused absences
D = Four unexcused absences

Improvement (10 percent)
Pretest − Posttest Score = Improvement Score
Improvement Score + Posttest Score = Improvement Grade for each skill test

Extra Credit.   Students who complete one intramural game make up one absence.

Teachers need to invest the time and effort necessary to establish an acceptable grading policy. Such a policy will prevent misunderstanding and disappointment when grades are issued. A structured, well-defined policy will eliminate some of the pressure that accompanies grade reporting.

Students need to understand that they are responsible for *earning* their grades.

Roll Call Procedure

Roll call procedures should be based on class size, facilities, departmental policy, and student age and gender. Roll call is a good time for teachers to make one-on-one contact with students. However, it should be completed accurately, without wasting time. The following methods have proven effective:

1. Ask students to form a line in alphabetical order by their last names. As they stand side by side, facing the teacher, they count off. (Teachers can number their alphabetical class lists to correspond, so that each student is always identified by the same number.) Teachers can also use this line formation with a nonverbal check by merely observing who is missing.
2. Paint numbers on the floor or blacktop and require students to stand on an assigned number. Empty numbers identify students who are absent.
3. Place a numbered board, with numbered tags attached by staple nails, in a central location. (The staple nail is used to attach the tag to the board so it cannot be removed—see figure 1.1.) Record roll call numbers on one side of each tag, leaving the other side blank. Students turn over their roll call number tags before reporting to class. Blank tags identify absent students.
4. Assign students to squads (see the following section). The squad leader or captain may then take roll and report to the teacher.

FIGURE   1.1
Staple Nail and Tag Used
on Roll Call Board.

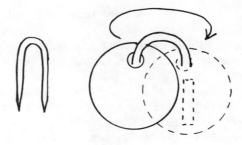

Creating Teams or Squads

In *most* cases, the teacher selects teams or squads and reorganizes them often. A rotation system is helpful. Teams or squads may be interchanged in the following ways:

1. The first two members and/or the last two members from each squad rotate one team to the right. The members on the last team to the right rotate to the first team.
2. The middle four members of each squad rotate as described in number 1.
3. Every other member of each squad rotates as described in number 1.

Students often want to elect team captains. If they do, the teacher is usually responsible for selecting the team members. Students may also take part in this decision by using one of the following methods:

1. Elected captains stand in front of the class. On command, students *walk* to stand behind the captain of their choice. When the designated number of team members is reached, students must choose another line.
2. Teacher and captains go to the teacher's office to select team members. Student captains are reminded that this is a confidential process.
3. The teacher calls for everyone with a birthday in a certain month, or with blue eyes or a green shirt, to stand in one line. This is a simple method and particularly effective in the elementary school. The creative teacher looks over the class to determine characteristics to be used in team selection.
4. Coed teams should be heterogeneously grouped with both boys and girls acting as team leaders.

Never allow student captains to stand in front of the class and select team members. The same students will usually be selected last each time this process is used.

Naming Teams or Squads

Be creative in identifying teams or squads. Team names can generate fun and excitement during competitive activities. Create your own team names or select from the following ideas:

1. Choose colors—the Red Team, the Gold Team, the Blue Team.
2. Select numbers—Team 1, Team 2, Team 3.
3. Select animal names—the Cougars, the Bears, the Lions.
4. Select bird names—the Hawks, the Robins, the Eagles.
5. Select names related to months of the year—for example, in October use the Witches, the Cats, the Pumpkins, and the Ghosts; in December, the Angels, the Reindeer, the Elves, and the Snowmen.
6. Let the students choose their own names—the Ziggies, the Winners, the Zombies.
7. Select names of professional teams—the Celtics, the Jazz, the Nuggets.

Class Formation for Instruction and Drills

Students should be taught the names and positioning for basic drills and patterns. They will then be able to move quickly to instructional formations. Selection of the proper formation enables all students to hear instructions and observe demonstrations.

FORMATION

1. Semicircle

```
        X  X
      X        X
    X            X
  X       T       X
```

2. Open Military

```
X X X X X X X X X X
  X X X X X X X X X
  X X X X X X X X X
```

Height

```
X   X   X   Tall
X   X   X   Medium
X   X   X   Short
```

APPLICATION

Teaching or demonstrating a new skill

Brief warm-ups, explanations

Eye contact for large groups

3. Line

Practice formation; teaching
or demonstrating a new skill

X X X X X X X

4. Double Line

Partner activities; moving
group from one place to
another

```
              T
X  X  X  X  X  X  X
X  X  X  X  X  X  X
```

```
        X     X
                 T
     X     X
   X     X
 X     X
```

Demonstrations
eye contact

5. Single File

Relays; marching

```
X
X
X
X
X
X
```

6. Columns (Several file lines)

Partner drill

```
X     X
X     X
X     X
X     X
X     X
X     X
```

7. Square or Circle

Drill formation; demo

```
O     O     O
O           O
O     O  T  O
```

How to Make Drills Motivational and Fun

Drill groups should be small enough to provide multiple turns for each group member. Otherwise, students will not meet the teacher's learning objectives. Optimum learning occurs when **no more than four to five students comprise a group.** Conduct group drills on a whistle command to allow observation of no more than six to eight players at a time.

Suggestions for successful drill participation include the following:

1. **BE ORGANIZED!** Have sufficient equipment. Distribute it quickly and efficiently so participation can begin without delay.
2. **BE ENTHUSIASTIC!** A disinterested teacher does not motivate students to practice.
3. **BE CREATIVE!** The creative use of hula hoops, cones, bowling pins, bean bags, jump ropes, beach balls, and flags can generate fun in various activities.
4. **ADAPT AND MODIFY!** Modify or adapt drills when necessary to increase participation and fun, improve skill, create competition, or overcome equipment and facility limitations.
5. **STOP BEFORE INTEREST WANES!** Change the drill often and prepare more drills than necessary. This enables the teacher to drop an activity that is not working and prevents stretching a poor drill to the end of the class period.
6. **USE CHALLENGING DRILLS!**
   a. Move from simple to advanced skills. For example, in basketball
      (1) pass and catch.
      (2) pivot, pass, and catch.
      (3) dribble, pass, and catch.
      (4) dribble, pivot, pass, and catch.
      (5) dribble, pass, and catch to a moving partner.
      (6) dribble, pivot, pass, and catch to a moving partner.
   b. Use a basic drill and vary the expectations.
      (1) Count consecutive executions.
      (2) Count executions in a designated time period.
      (3) Count executions from different positions (right, left).
      (4) Count moving executions.
      (5) Count game situation executions.

Organization and Distribution of Equipment

Issue equipment quickly to enhance class organization and provide additional time for instruction. Guidelines for efficient equipment distribution include the following:

1. **How**
   a. much equipment will be needed
   b. equipment will be issued

2. **Where**
   a. equipment will be issued and returned
3. **Who**
   a. will issue equipment
   b. will receive and return equipment

It is wise to number and label all pieces of equipment (for example, Windsor Elem., #5). This system allows easy identification of missing items.

   Suggested methods for organizing and distributing equipment include the following:

1. Equipment manager(s) may be appointed to put items in bags or carts for easy movement. These students should record how much equipment is issued, and account for all items at the end of class. Assign additional students to take out and return equipment for their group or team. Rotate this assignment so all students learn to care for and be responsible for equipment.
2. Instructors may distribute equipment, using student help when necessary. Students must receive clear instructions.
3. Students may check out their own equipment from a central place. A numbering system, using either of the following methods, could be used:
   a. Students may select a piece of equipment bearing their individual roll call number. Missing equipment can then be easily identified.
   b. Students may select a piece of equipment with any number. Record this number next to the student's roll call number. (These two numbers will usually be different.)

Shower Policy

Showers are optional in many physical education programs. If the class activity is vigorous enough, students will want to take showers or sponge off, especially if clean towels and facilities are available.

   When towels are not provided, students may opt to bring one from home. However, this can create problems if lockers are not ventilated to permit drying.

Safety Precautions

Most accidents are preventable! Student safety should be the paramount consideration of the instructor in planning all learning experiences. **Post** a list of enforceable safety rules in a conspicuous and visible place. Give a copy of these rules to all students and parents.

   The following rules are examples of what might be posted:

1. DO NOT run in the locker room and shower area.
2. DO NOT wear jewelry during any activity.

3. DO NOT participate in any activity in bare or stocking feet.
4. DO NOT play with broken or defective equipment.
5. DO NOT participate without protective equipment in sports that require it (for example, in softball, masks, chest protectors, and gloves; in hockey, shin guards).
6. DO NOT use equipment of the wrong size or weight such as a shot, javelin, bow, arrow, or bat.
7. DO NOT move heavy, over-sized equipment.
8. DO report any illness, accident, or abnormality immediately.

The teacher must also assume responsibility for a safe environment. These guidelines might prove helpful:

1. **Never leave a class unattended.**
2. Post emergency procedures.
3. To help avoid liability, record all details about accidents. Obtain the signatures of at least two witnesses, and file reports immediately in the school's administrative office.
4. Do not ignore the "goof-offs" in your class! Make sure they obey safety rules.
5. Keep dangerous equipment, such as trampolines, parallel bars, bows, arrows, fencing foils, javelin, and shots, behind locked doors when not in use. The swimming pool should also be locked when not supervised.
6. Identify the proper line of direction and spacing between participants involved in throwing and shooting.
7. Control the environment when dangerous implements, such as arrows, javelin, or shot are being used. Give **commands** for students to start and retrieve. Require those waiting their turns to stand well behind the participants.
8. Avoid facing students directly into the sun.
9. Deflate kickballs slightly until students learn safe kicking skills or when playing in the gymnasium.
10. Check facilities for unsafe conditions. Walk around outdoor facilities on a regular basis. Look for sinkholes, chuckholes, sprinkler heads, and wet grass.
11. Clear all playing areas of equipment not in use.
12. When playing softball, keep the batting team behind the backstop. If a backstop is not available, identify an appropriate, safe waiting area and keep the batting team in that area.
13. Use spotters for activities such as tumbling and gymnastics.
14. Mark all fields and playing areas with appropriate lines and sectors.
15. Close all doors, especially those opening into a playing area.
16. Do not allow students to perform skills without proper training and conditioning.

End-of-Class Procedures

School policy usually dictates whether students are permitted to leave the gymnasium complex before the bell rings. Make clear to students the specific rules or restrictions that exist in regard to class dismissal.

MOTIVATION TIPS

Motivation begins on the first day of class. **You, the teacher, are the prime motivator.** Don't expect your students to be excited about an activity when you are tentative or disinterested. Let each class know that you love the subject matter.

Learn Each Student's Name

Learn each student's name immediately. The following ideas may help the teacher recall student names:

1. Require students to write their names on their gym uniforms with permanent marker.
2. Take a photograph of the entire class, or of several small groups within the class. Label each student's name on the photo.
3. Ask students to state their names during the daily roll call until you commit each name to memory.
4. Assign each student a specific place identified on a chart. Make a conscientious effort to identify students by name.
5. Have each student fill out a short biography card. Match one piece of biographical information with each student's name and face.
6. Choose some personal characteristic to distinguish between twins, or to keep track of students with the same name.

Student Expectations

Cultivating positive habits helps motivate a class. From the first day of school, begin **training** students to respond immediately to directions and signals.

Teaching Moments

A physical education teacher is an educator first and foremost, and then a physical education specialist. The educator capitalizes on the teaching moment. This means that the teacher never lets a game or activity become so important that there is no time to deal with questions, problems, or unusual circumstances, or to recognize successful accomplishments as they occur. Deal with obscene language at the moment it occurs; likewise, compliment a good display of team work as you see it happen. These and similar situations merit immediate attention.

There are many times throughout the school year when administrative scheduling inadvertently cuts one or more class periods too short for regular instruction. A class shortened to fifteen minutes provides an opportune time to discuss the questionable display of sportsmanship that might have occurred at an athletic event the previous night. It might also be a good time to talk with students about being involved in, and supportive of, a variety of activities sponsored by the school.

Other Motivators

Once the teacher establishes the foregoing ideas as standard procedure, the class can be further enhanced by utilizing some additional motivation techniques. For example:

1. Give students a jogging ticket for each lap of the track they complete. Allow them to redeem tickets for make-up credit, extra points, or special recognition.
2. Use charts to record success and skill improvement.
3. Give awards for outstanding achievement over the year.
4. Use brightly painted equipment.
5. Maintain clean facilities and equipment.
6. Decorate the dressing room, locker room, and gymnasium with charts, thought-provoking statements, and posters.
7. Recognize student achievements in other school activities and award programs.

MAKING EQUIPMENT

It is rare to find a storage room stocked with all the necessary equipment to conduct a well-rounded program. Many items can be improvised, substituted, or constructed inexpensively by the creative teacher. The following section lists the basics for construction and adaptation of some pieces of equipment:

Track and Field

High Jump Crossbar	One-half-inch wide elastic (purchased from fabric store) attached to standards
	Bamboo pole
Relay Batons	Mailing tubes
	Newspapers rolled and wrapped with duct tape or masking tape

Starting Blocks	Partner's feet
	INSIDE: Wood blocks with rubber glued underneath—secure blocks with partners' feet
	OUTSIDE: Two blocks of wood with spikes placed into the middle of each block
Standing Long Jump	INSIDE: Tumbling mats for landing (must be secure so they won't slide)
	OUTSIDE: Dry, grassy area
Starting Signal	Two boards clapped together
	Whistle
Finish Line	Knitting yarn stretched across line
Field Markers	Plastic bottles filled with sand
	Tongue depressors, brightly painted or numbered, to identify where implements land
Hurdles	Dowel (purchased at lumber store) placed across two chairs (from backs of chairs to runners)
	Yardstick across two cones
Discus	Two sturdy paper or plastic plates taped together, with a bean bag inside

Softball

Ball	Tube socks rolled into a ball and turned inside out, with openings sewn shut
Bases	Carpet pieces cut to base dimensions

Recreational Games

Floor Targets	Hula hoops
	Rubber inner tubes (various sizes)
	Jump ropes formed into different shapes
	Water-based (washable) white shoe polish
	Carpet squares with the rubber side down
Small Balls	Newspapers wadded into balls and wrapped with masking tape
Badminton Shuttlecocks	Pom-poms (large size) purchased at craft store
	Yarn balls made from scraps
Bean Bags	Fabric remnants, such as denim, cut into four-by-four- or six-by-six-inch squares and sewn together with beans, corn, rice, or wheat inside (For lighter bags, fill with plastic pellets from an upholstery or craft store, cotton balls, or old nylons.)

Hula Hoops	One-inch-wide pliable plastic tubing (purchased from a plumbing or landscape supply store) cut into thirty-inch pieces and connected with a piece of dowel one inch wide and three inches long (staple tubing to dowel)
Paddle Rackets	One-quarter-inch duraply (purchased at the lumber yard) cut into the shape of a racquetball racket but with a shorter and narrower handle
Table-Tennis Tables	A piece of three-quarter-inch plywood cut five by ten feet; painted, lined, and attached to two ten-gallon, weighted garbage cans or two sawhorses
Scoops	Half-gallon plastic bottles cut to form a scoop
Blocks	Wood scraps of different shapes and sizes (collected from construction sites or cabinet mills) sanded and painted bright colors
Bowling Pins	Old pins collected from the local bowling alleys sanded, numbered, and painted bright colors
Scooters	Three-quarter-inch plywood cut into fourteen-by-fourteen-inch squares, sanded, painted bright colors, and mounted on two-inch swivel castors

Dance Equipment

Tinikling Poles	Two ten- or twelve-foot lengths of one- to two-inch lumber wrapped on each end with floor marking tape or cloth (Another option is two ten- or twelve-foot bamboo poles wrapped on each end with floor marking tape or cloth; use blocks instead of the floor for pole contact.)
Maori (Lumi) Sticks	One half-inch dowel cut in twelve-inch lengths, sanded, and painted or wrapped with floor marking tape on each end
Drum	Round cereal box, painted and turned upside down (beat with hand or stick)

Multiple-Use Equipment

Toss-Through Targets	Four-by-four-foot pieces of duraply or plywood cut with holes of various sizes and shapes (Cut at least four, and decorate with different backgrounds such as a clown, balloons, animals, or numbers.)
Barrels	Twenty- to fifty-gallon cardboard barrels, purchased from a storage or barrel company, opened at each end and painted bright colors
Ball Cart	A twenty-gallon plastic garbage can bolted at each corner to a scooter
Jump Ropes	Three-quarter-inch nylon cord cut in eight- and ten-foot lengths (Singe the ends to prevent unraveling.)
Wands	Thirty-six-inch lengths of one-by-one-inch pine lumber, sanded and painted bright colors
Standards	A three-inch-wide metal pole, nine feet in length, cemented in the center of a small auto tire (Cut a wood base to be placed inside the tire before pouring cement. Drill holes in the pole and attach hooks at appropriate heights for a net or crossbars.)
Team Shirts	White T-shirts donated by students; remove sleeves, add numbers, and dye bright colors
	White tank-top male underwear, numbered and dyed bright colors

CHAPTER TWO

BADMINTON

Badminton is a singles or doubles racket game suitable for people of any age or skill level. It is especially appropriate for coed play. To the highly skilled, it is a game of speed, strategy, and taxing cardiovascular endurance. For the inexperienced player, it is generally a social game requiring moderate exercise and minimum skill.

EQUIPMENT

Indoor plastic shuttlecocks
Feather shuttlecocks
Rackets
Nets/Standards

SUGGESTIONS FOR INSTRUCTIONAL PROFICIENCY

1. Provide enough rackets for everyone in the class, or rotate to allow students equal racket time.
2. Ask students to protect the equipment, and stress that rackets be used only to hit the shuttlecocks. Show students how to manicure a feathered shuttlecock.
3. Expect students to retrieve shuttlecocks and return rackets. Request students to report damaged or broken equipment.
4. Provide enough shuttlecocks for students to continuously practice. Store sufficient inventory to allow for damage and loss.
5. Use the shuttlecock designed for the setting students are in—either outdoor or indoor play. The class may also use shuttlecocks especially designed for high, moderate, and slow speeds.
6. Make sure that students practicing in confined areas have sufficient room to swing the racket.
7. Teach beginning lessons without nets. Allow students to practice clearing, smashing, and hitting for wrist action when space is limited and when hand-eye coordination is the objective.
8. Teach the rules and strategy along with the skills, drills, and lead-up games.
9. Introduce the regulation game when students are able to keep the shuttlecock in play.
10. Play short games, switching partners and courts often, to enhance motivation and involve large numbers of students.

TEACHING THE BASICS

The following progression is suggested:

1. **Preliminary Actions**

   Grip
   Swish swing: Swing the racket with enough *wrist action* to hear the "swish"
      of the racket.
   Upsies: Hold the racket head above the waist and hit the shuttlecock over
      and over again to a height of approximately two feet above the racket
      head.

2. **Stroke Practice:** Partners face each other, approximately twelve to fifteen feet
   apart, to practice these skills. Nets and standards are not required in the
   beginning phase.

   Underhand clear (forehand, backhand)
   Overhead clear (forehand, backhand)
   Alternate forehand/backhand (good for footwork)
   Serve: short, long
   Smash
   Net shots

3. **Regulation Court Play:** Practice strokes or game situations on the court with the
   net.

   Rules
   Strategy
   Side-by-side
   Up and back
   Rotation

DRILLS

The following drill, "Sixies," is suggested practice for any stroke at the beginner level.
Nets and standards may be used but are not required. Three people on each side of
the court rally the shuttlecock, using any or all the skills learned. One player on each
side is back, and the other two players are at the net, or vice versa. Various scoring
methods may be used; for example, a point might be awarded to the side that does not
commit an error.

Clear

Wall Clear

Stand approximately six feet from a wall and hit the shuttlecock continuously above a net-high line.

(Court)   1   2   3

```
            B                 H              N

      A    C      G        I        M    O
      _____

      _____

          D    F      J     L        P    R

             E              K              Q
```

Underhand Clear (Figure 2.1)

1. Partners stand on opposite sides of the net directly across from each other.
2. One partner puts the shuttlecock in play with an underhand hit. Practice any of the following strokes
   a. Forehand
   b. Backhand
   c. Forehand and backhand alternately
3. The partner on the other side of the net returns the shuttlecock with an underhand clear.

FIGURE   2.1

Underhand and Overhead Clear.

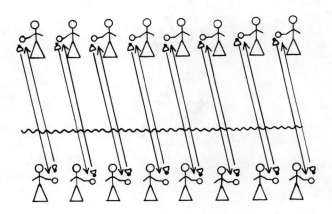

4. Play continues until an error is committed.
5. The shuttlecock is once again put into play with an underhand hit.
6. Count the number of continuous hits without an error.
7. Move back one step after each hit until the shuttlecock comes down in the back of the court.
8. Hit forehand and backhand when appropriate.

Overhead Clear

1. Use the same progression as in the underhand clear.
2. Alternate underhand and overhead clears.

Forehand/Backhand Clear (Figure 2.2)

1. Hit overhead and underhand clears using only the forehand.
2. Hit overhead and underhand clears using only the backhand.
3. Hit overhead and underhand clears using forehand and backhand when appropriate.

Short Serve/Long Serve

The following drills are appropriate for the short or the long serve.

Straight Serve (Figure 2.3)

1. Partners stand on opposite sides of the center line directly across from each other. No net is necessary. (Six players can practice at the same time.)
2. Servers serve across the center line.
3. Receivers allow the shuttlecock to drop in the court.

FIGURE   2.2
Forehand/Backhand Clear.

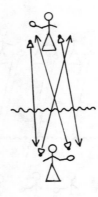

FIGURE   2.3
Straight Serve.

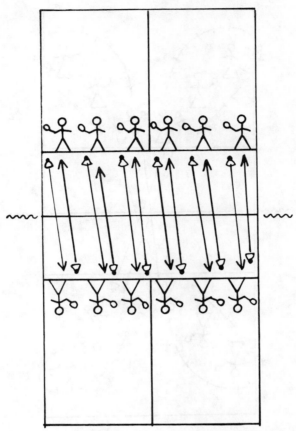

4. Receivers pick up the shuttlecock and serve it back.
5. Receivers move back when servers practice the long serve.
6. Add the net when students show serving competency.

Diagonal Serve (Figure 2.4)

1. Partners stand diagonally across from one another on opposite sides of the net. (Four to six players can practice at the same time.)
2. Servers direct the shuttlecock diagonally across the net.
3. Receivers allow the shuttlecock to drop in the court before serving the shuttlecock back.
4. Each server moves to the end of a line of waiting players to again rotate to the serving position.
5. Receivers move back when servers practice the long serve.

FIGURE   2.4
Diagonal Serve.

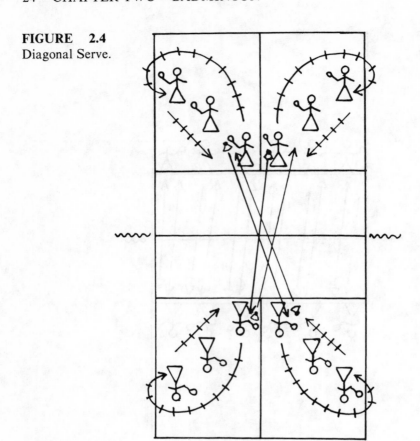

Continuous Serve (Figure 2.5)

1. Two to six servers position themselves in diagonal lines on one side of the court. Receivers are positioned on the opposite side of the court.
2. Each person on the service side of the net begins with five shuttlecocks.
3. Allow players to serve all five shuttlecocks.
4. Players on the opposite side of the net collect five shuttlecocks each and form diagonal lines to serve them back.
5. Receivers move back when servers practice the long serve.
6. Repeat the process when all shuttlecocks have been served.

FIGURE   2.5
Continuous Serve.

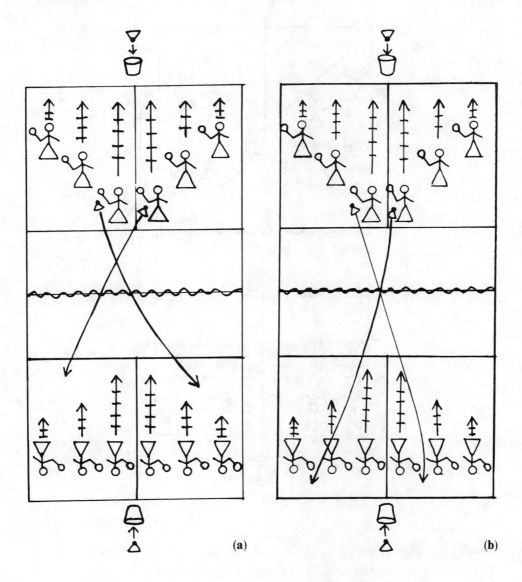

(a)   (b)

FIGURE   2.6
Serving for Accuracy.

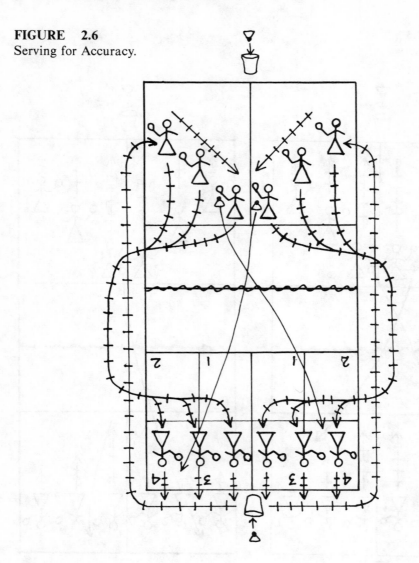

Serve for Accuracy (Figure 2.6)

1. Partners stand diagonally across the net.
2. Servers aim for specific, marked areas of the court.
3. When all shuttlecocks have been served, partners switch sides of the court.
   (This means that targets must only be laid out on one side.)
4. The other partners repeat the process.

FIGURE   2.7
The Short Serve.

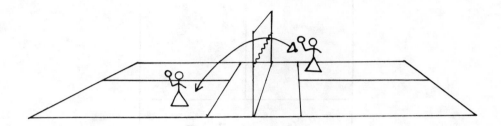

Short-Serve-Technique Perfection (Figure 2.7)

1. String a cord twelve to eighteen inches above the net.
2. Partners stand diagonally across the net.
3. The served shuttlecock must travel between the cord and the net and land in the short service area.
4. Partners alternate serving the shuttlecock.

Smash

Basketball Target Smash

1. Assign five students to each basketball net.
2. Student take turns reaching high to strike the basketball net with their rackets. (The net represents a stationary shuttlecock.)

Partner Toss-and-Hit Smash

1. Partner tosses (or hits) the shuttlecock high.
2. Receiver points free arm and hand at the shuttlecock in flight.
3. Receiver hits a smash.
4. After five hits, partners change positions.

Net Shots

Hairpin (Figure 2.8)

1. Partners stand opposite each other and close to the net.
2. One partner puts the shuttlecock in play. Players count the number of continuous hairpin shots performed.

FIGURE   2.8
The Hairpin.

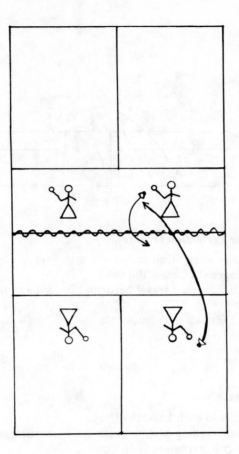

Drop Shot

1. Partners stand opposite each other in the middle of the court. (Two to six players may be on one court.)
2. One partner puts the shuttlecock in play with a toss or hit three to four feet above the net.
3. The receiver performs a drop shot, lightly tapping the shuttlecock at contact, causing it to drop sharply down toward the floor.

Footwork Drills

Group Footwork

1. The teacher, holding the racket in ready position, faces the class and directs their movement with the racket head.
2. On the command "go," students move to the cues provided by the teacher. Action cues follow:
   a. Racket head up: Students run forward, holding rackets in ready position.
   b. Racket head left: Students slide left.
   c. Racket head right: Students slide right.
   d. Racket head forward: Students hold rackets in ready position and back pedal.
3. A vocal command or whistle signals the group to stop.

Individual Footwork (Figure 2.9)

1. Divide players into equal groups on each half court.
2. One player on each half court starts in the left front (*A* in figure 2.9) in ready position with racket head held up.
3. The instructor signals players to begin.
4. The first player slides to the right alley (*B* in figure 2.9).
5. When the player reaches the right alley (*B*), he or she back pedals diagonally to the left back corner (*C* in figure 2.9).
6. From the left back corner, the player slides to the right back corner (*D* in figure 2.9) and then runs diagonally forward to starting position (*A*).
7. This process is continued until all students have had an equal number of turns.
8. On the opposite side of the court, students perform the same footwork pattern in the opposite direction (*B* to *A* to *D* to *C*).

Variation on Individual Footwork (Figure 2.10)

After reaching the final position (*D* in one half-court, *C* in the other), slide behind the baseline and along the sideline to return to the starting point (*A* or *B*).

FIGURE   2.9
Individual Footwork.

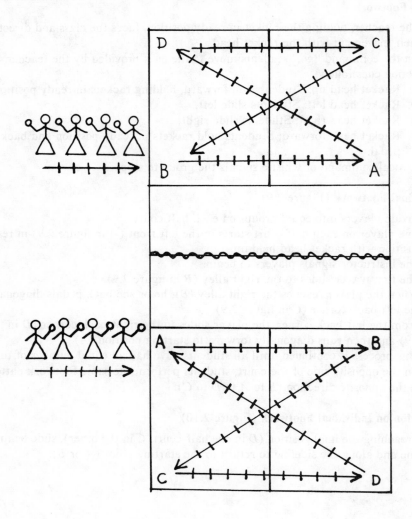

FIGURE   2.10
Variation on Individual Footwork.

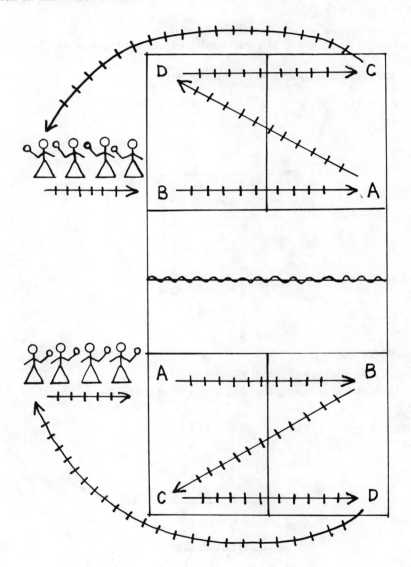

Pregame Warm-ups

Wall Clear (Figure 2.11)

1. Player stands six to eight feet from the wall.
2. The player continuously hits the shuttlecock against the wall above a net-high line.
3. All strokes may be practiced from this position.

FIGURE   2.11
Wall Clear.

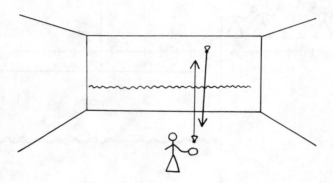

Partner Wall Clear (Figure 2.12)

1. Follow directions for the Wall Clear drill.
2. Partners alternate hitting the shuttlecock after it hits the wall.

FIGURE   2.12
Partner Wall Clear.

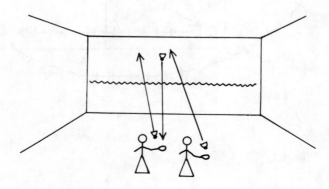

Shuttle Wall Clear (Figure 2.13)

1. Players line up in file formation facing a wall. The leader stands six to eight feet from the wall.
2. The leader hits the shuttlecock against the wall above a net-high line.
3. The leader moves to the right and to the end of the shuttle line.
4. The next player in line hits the shuttlecock and moves to the end of the line.
5. Play continues in this manner until all players hit the shuttlecock a designated number of times.
6. Practice all strokes using this drill.

FIGURE   2.13
Shuttle Wall Clear.

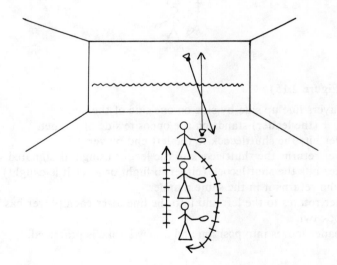

Six-Player Shuttle (Figure 2.14)

1. Three players line up in file formation on each side of the net.
2. The lead player in one line hits the shuttlecock over the net, then moves to the right and to the end of the shuttle line.
3. The lead player on the opposite side of the net returns the shuttlecock, then moves to the left and to the end of the line.
4. Play continues in this manner until all players hit the shuttlecock a designated number of times.
5. Practice all strokes using this drill.

FIGURE   2.14
Six-Player Shuttle.

Line Clear (Figure 2.15)

1. Three players line up side-by-side on one side of the net.
2. One player (the leader) stands on the opposite side of the net.
3. The leader hits the shuttlecock to the left-end player.
4. The player returns the shuttlecock to the leader using a designated stroke.
5. The leader hits the shuttlecock (either in flight or after it is caught) to the next player, who returns it in the same manner.
6. The leader rotates to the left and into the line after each player has hit the shuttlecock twice.
7. A new leader moves into position and a new stroke is practiced.

FIGURE   2.15
Line Clear Warm-up.

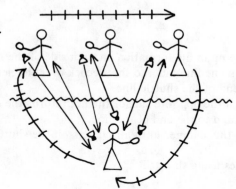

LEAD-UP GAMES

Fleeceball Badminton

Beginners enjoy this game because it gives them a feel for badminton. It is not played to perfect strokes or strategies.

Equipment

Regulation court, rackets, fleeceball

Procedures (Figure 2.16)

1. Four (or more) players take each court, with two players in the forecourt and two players in the backcourt.
2. Right back player puts the fleeceball into play. Then the game is played and scored like volleyball.
3. If extra players remain, they rotate onto the court and replace on-court players after each serve.

FIGURE   2.16
Fleeceball Badminton.

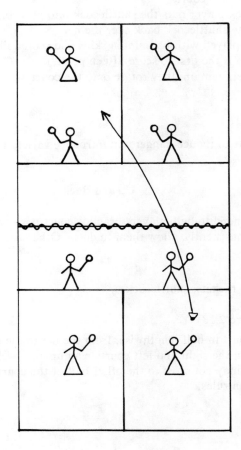

Variations

1. Front players only hit forehand and back players only hit backhand (or vice versa).
2. Dividing the court lengthwise, players on the right hit backhand shots while those on the left hit forehand shots (or vice versa).

Team Badminton

This game is played for enjoyment and for total class participation.

Equipment

Regulation court, rackets, shuttlecock

Procedures (Figure 2.17)

1. Six players take each court, with three players in the forecourt and three players in the backcourt.
2. The right back player puts the shuttlecock into play. Each team is allowed one hit to send the shuttlecock back over the net.
3. The game is played with badminton skills and scored like volleyball (the winning team is the first to score fifteen points).
4. If extra players remain, they rotate onto the court and replace on-court players after each serve.

Variation

Use shorty rackets to reduce danger and introduce variety to the game.

Up and Back

This game is intended to help players practice court positioning. If players can serve the shuttlecock consistently, allow them to do so. Otherwise, toss it into play.

Equipment

Regulation court, rackets, shuttlecock

Procedures (Figure 2.18)

1. Divide the court in half lengthwise, from the net to the baseline.
2. The players in the right and left courts play up and back in their respective half courts. They may not cross to the other half of the court to play the shuttlecock.
3. Use regulation rules.

FIGURE   2.17
Team Badminton.

FIGURE   2.18
Up and Back.

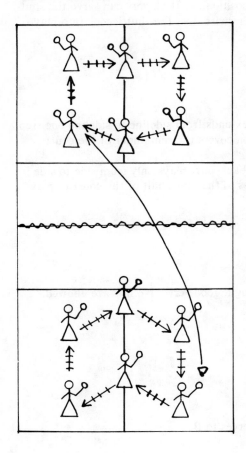

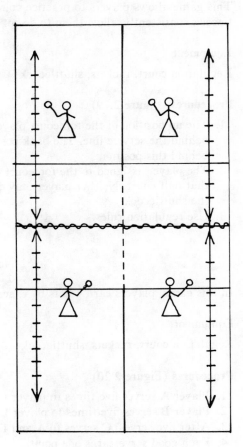

Side to Side

This game allows players to practice court positioning. If players can serve the shuttlecock consistently, allow them to do so. Otherwise, toss the shuttlecock into play.

Equipment

Regulation court, rackets, shuttlecock

Procedures (Figure 2.19)

1. The **up** position of the forecourt player extends from sideline to sideline one step behind the service line. The **back** position covers the remainder of the court behind this position.
2. The player assigned to the forecourt or backcourt plays only from side to side in that half court. Neither player may cross to the other half of the court to play the shuttlecock.
3. Use regulation rules.

No Hit

In this game, players earn points by executing a good serve. **No hits are allowed.**

Equipment

Regulation court, rackets, shuttlecock

Procedures (Figure 2.20)

1. Player A serves five times to player C.
2. Player B serves five times to player D.
3. After five serves, C serves to A and D serves to B.
4. Each good serve earns one point.
5. The team to score the most points, or the most points during a designated time period, wins the game.

FIGURE   2.19
Side to Side.

FIGURE   2.20
No Hit.

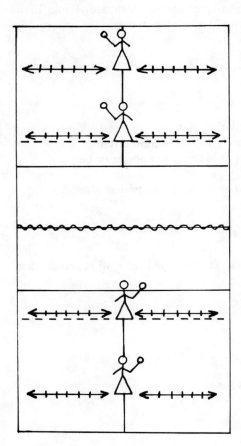

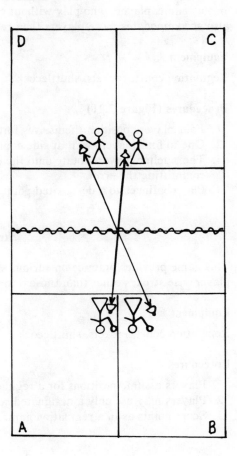

Triple Team

In this game, players who play without committing errors are rewarded. Triple Team also accommodates more players than regulation badminton allows.

Equipment

Regulation court, rackets, shuttlecock

Procedures (Figure 2.21)

1. Four players position themselves for regulation play.
2. One to four players wait at side court until an error is committed.
3. The sideline players rotate onto the court in place of the player or players committing the error.
4. Play continues to a designated point total or for a certain period of time.

Stroke It

This game provides practice on various strokes. The opposing team wins points when players use strokes other than those designated.

Equipment

Regulation court, rackets, shuttlecock

Procedures

1. Players assume positions for a regulation game.
2. Players may use only a designated stroke or strokes.
3. Score points as in a regulation game.

FIGURE   2.21
Triple Team.

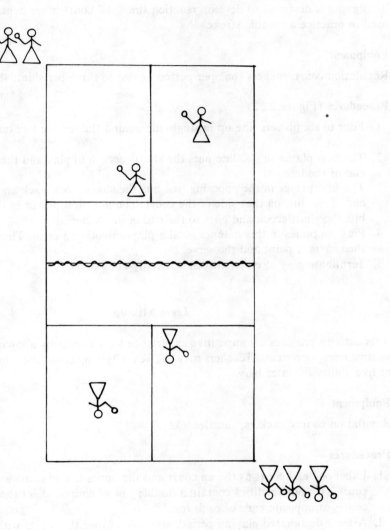

Progressive Badminton

This game is designed to develop reaction time and court movement. It may also be used to practice a specific stroke.

Equipment

Regulation court, rackets (one per person or two to three per side), shuttlecocks

Procedures (Figure 2.22)

1. Four to six players line up in single file behind the service line on each side of the net.
2. The first player in one line puts the shuttlecock into play and then goes to the end of the line.
3. The first player in the opposing line hits the shuttlecock back and goes to the end of the line on that side of the court. The new first player in the opposite line hits the shuttlecock and goes to the end of his or her line.
4. Play continues in this manner until a player makes an error. The opposing team then earns a point and the serve.
5. Terminate play at either fifteen or twenty-one points.

Team Mix-up

This activity provides a competitive experience for students by allowing them to play against many opponents. Teachers may use Team Mix-up to aid them in pairing players of like ability for later play.

Equipment

Regulation courts, rackets, shuttlecocks

Procedures

1. Label one end court as the **up** court and the opposite end court as the **down** court. (If your facilities contain a double row of courts, select the up and down courts at opposite ends of each row.)
2. After a designated playing period, stop play. Move the teams with the higher scores in each game one court closer to the up court. (The only exception is the winning team on the up court—this team remains on the up court.)
3. The teams with the lower scores in each game remain on the same court. (The only exception is the losing team on the up court—this team rotates to the down court.)

FIGURE   2.22
Progressive Badminton.

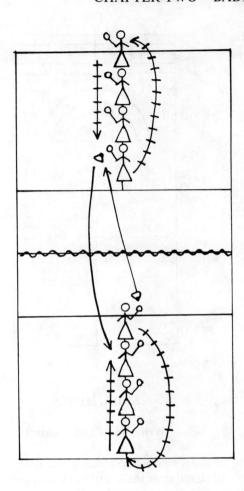

Variations

1. When play stops, all teams move one court to the right. In this variation, longer playing periods are desirable, so teams don't repeatedly play against the same opponents.
2. When play stops, each partner moves a half court to the right. Partners change for each game.

FIGURE   2.23
Short/Long Serve.

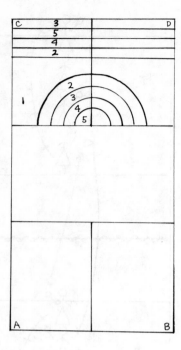

SKILL TESTS

Wrist Snap and Control

The player stands behind a six-foot restraining line and hits the shuttlecock continuously against the wall. Each time the shuttlecock drops to the floor, the player begins counting again. Record the highest number of continuous hits in thirty seconds.

Short/Long Serve (Figure 2.23)

Short Serve

Attach a string to the standards twelve to eighteen inches above the net. The player hits ten serves from each service court, attempting to send the shuttlecock between the rope and the net. Each serve must land within one of the short-serve target areas (lines placed twelve to eighteen inches apart and marked with point values, as shown in figure 2.23). The player serves the shuttlecock diagonally across the net, attempting to place five serves to the right side of the short-serve target area and five to the left side. The player's score is the total number of points accumulated. Liners count the higher number of points.

Long Serve

Set up a restraining rope seven feet in front of the end of the court and eight feet high (or assign a person to stand seven feet in front of the end line with a racket extended straight up) as a marker for the shuttlecock to clear. The player hits ten serves diagonally across the net and above the marker to the long-serve target area in the back of the court (lines placed twelve to eighteen inches apart and marked with point values, as shown in figure 2.23). The score is the total number of points accumulated by the shuttlecock traveling above the marker and landing inside the target court. Liners count the higher number of points.

Overhead Clear

Use the same court markings and restraining marker as used for the long-serve test. Players hit ten overhead clears to the back of the court. The player stands with one foot behind the doubles back service line and, with the hand or racket, tosses the shuttlecock in the air. The player then attempts to hit an overhead forehand clear over the marker and across the net. Liners count the higher number of points. The score is the total number of points accumulated.

Smash

A player stands in the center of the court and returns ten good overhead clears with a smash each time. (Poor clears are hit again.) Each smash that is returned in good form, with high speed, counts five points. Each smash that is returned in acceptable form, with medium speed, counts three points. Each smash that lands outside the singles court or is not hit with acceptable form or speed counts zero points. A skilled individual hits the overhead clears and determines the number of points awarded for each smash.

General Play

Using a checklist, the teacher evaluates the general playing ability of each student. The teacher then awards from one to five points for each player's execution in the following categories:

TECHNIQUE	POINTS
Wrist Snap	
Court Coverage (position, recovery)	
Placement (to opponent)	
Speed	
Net Shot Execution	
Drop Shot Execution	
Variation of Shots	

WRITTEN TEST

PART I. GAME SITUATIONS: Indicate the official's decision for each situation.

KEY: PC = Play continues
O = Side out
P = Point

_____ 1. The server performs a legal serve and the receiver fails to return the shuttle.

_____ 2. The serve falls on the short service line of the opponents' court.

_____ 3. The serving team hits the shuttlecock before it crosses their side of the net.

_____ 4. A receiver hits the shuttlecock, while in play, with the racket frame.

_____ 5. The server fails to move to the opposite side of the court after the first serve.

_____ 6. The server returns the shuttlecock from outside the court boundaries into the receiver's court.

_____ 7. The receiver's racket follows the shuttlecock over the net while the shuttlecock is in play.

_____ 8. During the service, the server's partner makes preliminary movements.

_____ 9. The receiving players hit the shuttlecock twice in succession while the shuttlecock is in play.

_____ 10. During play, the server's partner accidently touches the net.

_____ 11. During play, the shuttlecock is momentarily held on the receiver's racket.

_____ 12. Two hands down.

_____ 13. During the act of serving, the server fails to keep both feet in the service court before contacting the shuttlecock.

_____ 14. The server swings and misses a shuttlecock that falls out-of-bounds during play.

_____ 15. During play, the server hits a smash to the receiver's feet.

PART II. SKILL IDENTIFICATION: The vertical line in each diagram represents the net. Using arrows, diagram the flight of the shuttlecock for each skill.

Clear

Smash

Hairpin

Drop (overhead)

Drive

PART III. KNOWLEDGE OF THE COURT: Diagram a badminton court. Shade one side to indicate the singles service area and mark it *A*. Shade the other side to indicate the doubles service area and mark it *B*.

TEST KEY

1. P	4. PC	7. PC	10. O	13. O
2. P	5. O	8. O	11. P	14. P
3. O	6. PC	9. P	12. O	15. P

CHAPTER THREE

BASKETBALL

Basketball, an American creation, has been played by both men and women since its introduction in 1891. In the past century, the game has gained worldwide popularity. This sport requires cardiovascular endurance, individual ball handling skills, and co-operative teamwork.

EQUIPMENT

Basketballs
Vests or pinnies (colored)
Playing area with baskets and backboards
Practice materials: cones, stopwatch, whistles, game clock

SUGGESTIONS FOR INSTRUCTIONAL PROFICIENCY

1. Provide at least one regulation ball for every four people. Use the smaller regulation ball for girls.
2. Conduct drills and practice situations that develop endurance.
3. Begin play after students are adequately warmed up.
4. Don't allow students to bounce, sit on, or handle the balls while you are conducting demonstrations.
5. Use all available baskets and playing space for practice and play.
6. Teach accurate game rules and demonstrate all fouls and violations.
7. Emphasize scorekeeping and officiating techniques as a vital part of the game. Use students as scorekeepers and officials.
8. Reserve leather balls for inside play.

TEACHING THE BASICS

The following progression is suggested:

1. **Passing and Catching**: Instruct students in both skills simultaneously.

   Chest pass
   Bounce pass
   One-hand underhand pass
   Overhead passes
     One hand (Baseball)
     Two hand
   Hook pass

2. **Dribble**: Teach students to dribble with each hand.
3. **Pivot**: Teach pivoting on the right and left foot.
4. **Shooting and Rebounding:** Teach shooting and rebounding fundamentals at the same time. Require students to practice shooting from all areas of the court using *bank* and *rim* shots when appropriate.

   Two-handed push shot (elementary and less-skilled students)
   One-handed push shot
   Lay-up shot
   Free-throw shot
   Jump shot
   Hook shot

Students should also become proficient at combining skills:

5. **Dribble and Pass**
6. **Pass and Shoot**
7. **Dribble and Shoot**
8. **Dribble, Pass, and Shoot**
9. **Court Play:** Integrate the following skills and rules into a competitive game situation.

   Offensive tactics
   Defensive tactics
     Man-to-man
     Zone
       1–4
       2–3

Dribble, pass, and shoot over defenders
Feinting
Putting the ball into play
   Jump balls
   Out-of-bounds
Fouls
Violations

DRILLS

Pass and Catch

Wall Pass (Figure 3.1)

1. Each student with a ball stands four to six feet from the wall.
2. Students practice the techniques of a particular pass against the wall for a designated time or number of passes.
3. Resume practice with a different pass or with a different player repeating the same pass.

Partner Pass (Figure 3.2)

1. Partners face each other approximately ten to fifteen feet apart.
2. Partners practice the techniques of a particular pass as they pass the ball back and forth.

FIGURE   3.1
Wall Pass.

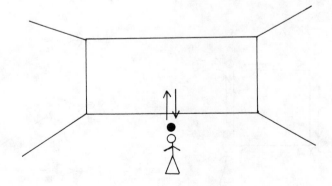

FIGURE   3.2
Partner Pass.

Box Pass (Figure 3.3)

1. Four players stand at each corner of a box six to ten feet square (vary the distance according to the players' skill).
2. Players pass the ball either clockwise or counterclockwise using a specific pass.
3. The player who catches the pass pivots and passes the ball to the next person.
4. Conclude the drill after a designated time or number of passes.

Variation

Incorporate a specific sequence of passes, changing the pass with each person or each time around the box. (For example, one sequence might be bounce pass, baseball, chest, then overhead.)

Zigzag Pass (Figure 3.4)

1. Six or more players form two parallel lines standing side by side at least three feet apart. (In a large class, form several groups of six to ten.)
2. The first player starts by passing the ball straight across to the first person in the opposite line.
3. The person catching the ball throws it across diagonally to the next person in the opposite line. Each player repeats this pattern.

FIGURE   3.3
Box Pass.

FIGURE   3.4
Zigzag Pass.

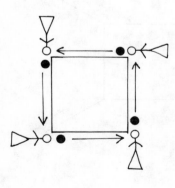

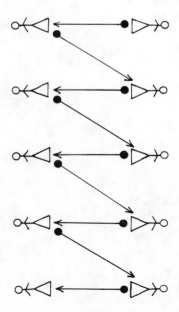

4. When the ball reaches the end of the line, the last person throws it straight across to the last person in the other line. This person sends it back diagonally, and the pattern is then repeated back to the start.

Variations

1. Several balls may be positioned next to the first person passing the ball. After three people have received and passed, the first person can start another ball along the line. When the last player receives the ball, he or she dribbles to the front of the line, becomes the new first person, and repeats the pattern.
2. For advanced players: The first person in the line may start a second ball when the first ball has reached the middle of the group. The person at the end of the line must return the balls back through the line. The players in the middle must be alert so as not to simultaneously pass two balls to the same person.

Circle Pass (Figure 3.5)

1. Six or eight players form a circle.
2. Players pass the ball back and forth across the circle, avoiding passes to the players on either side of the passer.
3. The drill is complete after a designated number of errorless passes or a designated time period.

Variation

Change the type of pass practiced after a designated number of successful completions.

FIGURE   3.5
Circle Pass.

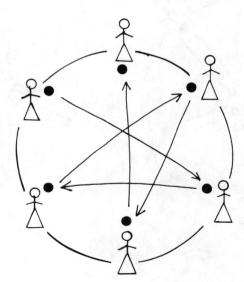

Center Circle Pass (Figure 3.6)

1. Six or eight players form a circle. Another player is assigned to the center.
2. The player in the center passes the ball to a receiver on the outside, who in turn quickly passes the ball back to the center.
3. The center player repeats the process with each player in the circle.
4. The center player changes positions with the first receiver once the ball has gone around to all players.

Variations

1. Vary the pass each time a new center comes in.
2. Vary the pass on command.

Circle In-Out Pass (Figure 3.7)

1. Six or eight players form a circle. Another player is assigned to the center.
2. One player on the *outside* of the circle (*S* in figure 3.7) passes into the center and then follows the ball by running into the center.

FIGURE   3.6
Center Circle Pass.

FIGURE   3.7
Circle In-Out Pass.

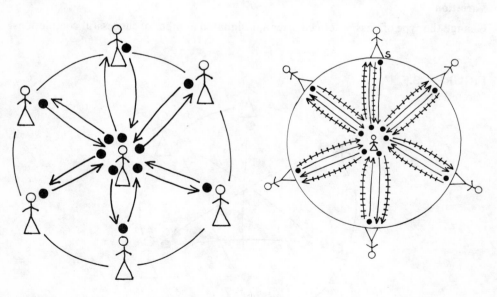

3. The receiving player in the center passes the ball clockwise to the next player on the outside of the circle. Then the center player follows the ball by running to the outside to take the place of that receiver.
4. The original outside player running to the center has now arrived there. Passing continues from center to outside and from outside to center. With each pass, the passer follows the ball by running to take the place of the receiver just passed to.
5. Play is stopped or the pass is changed when all players are back in their original places.

Star Pass (Figure 3.8)

1. Five players form a large circle.
2. One player passes across the circle, skipping the nearest clockwise neighbor and passing to the next player.
3. Each receiver repeats the same action. (To avoid confusion, give each player a number. Number 1 passes to number 3, number 3 to 5, 5 to 2, 2 to 4, and 4 to 1.)
4. Five passes completes a star pattern. The originator of the pass once again has the ball and can continue practicing the same pass or change to another.

FIGURE   3.8
Star Pass.

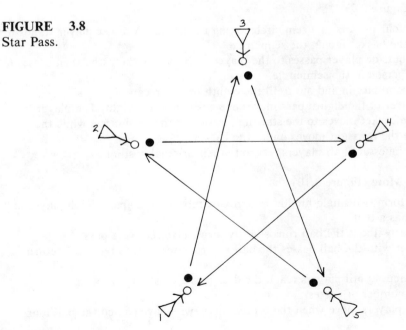

FIGURE 3.9
Eight Pass.

FIGURE 3.10
Partner Pass-Move.

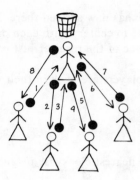

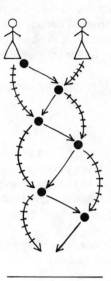

Eight Pass (Figure 3.9)

1. Arrange four players in a semicircle facing the basket. Another player stands in front of the basket facing the semicircle.
2. The left outside player passes to the player under the basket, who then passes to the next person in the semicircle.
3. Passing continues in and out until the eighth pass is received.
4. The receiver of the eighth pass moves one position to the right. The player under the basket moves to the starting position in the semi-circle while the player on the far right moves under the basket.
5. Play continues until all players return to their original positions.

Partner Pass-Move (Figure 3.10)

1. Partners form two single-file lines approximately six feet apart. Each player in one line has a ball.
2. The player without the ball runs slightly forward to receive a pass.
3. The player with the ball passes the ball and runs forward to receive a return pass.
4. Play continues until players reach the designated finish line or complete a specified number of passes.
5. Two new players move when the preceding players have passed the ball four times.
6. After players have crossed the finish line, they line up ready to execute the drill in the opposite direction.

FIGURE   3.11
Move-and-Pass Shuttle.

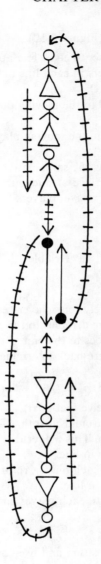

Move-and-Pass Shuttle (Figure 3.11)

1. Two shuttle lines face each other approximately twenty feet apart.
2. The player with the ball passes straight ahead to the opposing player as that player moves toward the ball.
3. The passer runs to the end of the opposite line.
4. Play continues until each player is back in starting position.

Three-Player Weave (Grapevine) (Figure 3.12)

1. Players form three file lines six to eight feet apart. The player in the center line holds the ball. The first players in each line move in a weaving pattern down the court (either half or full court).
2. The center player first passes to the moving player on the right and then runs behind this player.
3. The new ball handler passes to the moving player on the left and runs behind this player.
4. The players continue to follow the same pattern, passing right and then left.
5. After a group of three has arrived at midcourt, another threesome begins.
6. As each group completes the weave, players form three new lines to execute the drill in the opposite direction.

Dribble

Straight-Line Dribble

1. Form file lines of approximately four players each along the end lines.
2. The first player from each line dribbles to the center line and back, hands the ball to the next player, and goes to the end of the line.
3. Play continues until players are back to original positions.

Figure Eight Dribble (Figure 3.13)

1. Station five players ten to twelve feet apart.
2. The starting player dribbles around the other four players, weaving back and forth in a figure-eight pattern. This player dribbles back to the starting position, then passes to the next player in line.
3. The receiver dribbles around each player, returns to his or her place of origin, and passes to the next player in line.
4. Players repeat the pattern until each player completes the course.

Variation

Line players up at the starting position and use cones to mark the dribbling course. The player with the ball returns to the starting position and the next player begins.

FIGURE   3.12
Three-Player Weave.

FIGURE   3.13
Figure Eight Dribble.

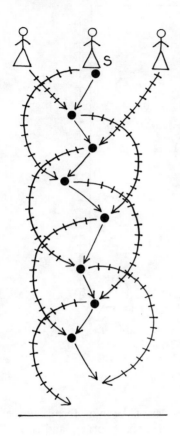

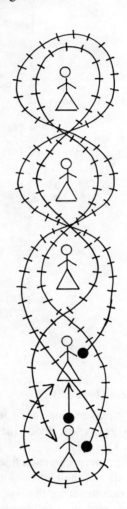

FIGURE 3.14
Box Dribble.

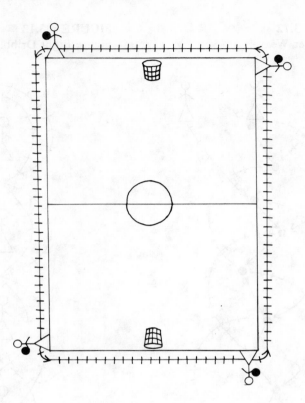

Box Dribble (Figure 3.14)

1. Divide players into four equal lines at each corner of the gym, forming a box. (In large classes, divide the gym in half and utilize eight corners and two boxes.)
2. The first player in each line takes a ball.
3. On a signal, the players with the balls dribble around the gym from corner to corner, completing the box formation.
4. Players returning to their original positions go to the end of the line.
5. Repeat the action until all players have had a turn.

FIGURE   3.15
Variation on the Box
Dribble: Hourglass
Dribble.

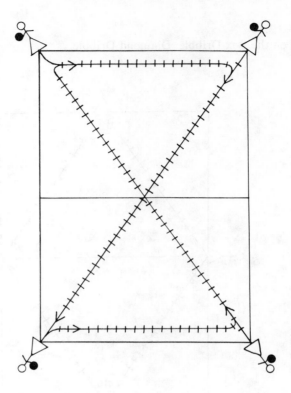

Variations

1. **Hourglass Dribble** (Figure 3.15): Line players up as for the Box Dribble.
   Players on one side of the gym begin by moving diagonally across the box, while
   players on the opposite side of the gym begin by moving straight across the end
   lines. When the four dribbling players complete the "hourglass" formation, they
   each give the ball to the next person and go to the end of their respective lines.
   Caution players to avoid each other at midcourt.
2. **Diamond Dribble** (Figure 3.16): To begin the drill, players shift from the
   corners of the box to midway between, as if they were standing at the corners of
   a diamond. Players then dribble diagonally across each quadrant of the box,
   completing the diamond.

FIGURE   3.16
Variation on the Box Dribble: Diamond Dribble.

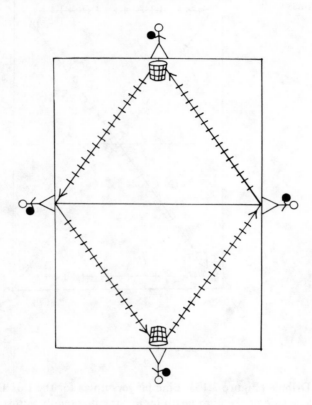

Circle Dribble (Figure 3.17)

1. Station six players approximately eight feet apart around a circle.
2. The player with the ball dribbles with the right hand completely around the outside of the circle, returning to starting position.
3. The first player passes to the player on the left, and this player repeats the process.
4. When each player has completed the drill, the players repeat it, reversing direction and dribbling with the left hand.

FIGURE   3.17
Circle Dribble.

FIGURE   3.18
Five-Ball Circle Dribble.

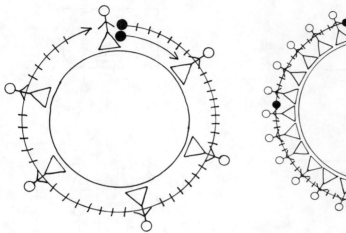
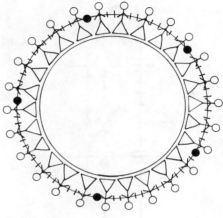

Five-Ball Circle Dribble (Figure 3.18)

1. Position the entire class in a circle with five balls distributed evenly among the students.
2. On a signal, players with the balls begin dribbling counterclockwise around the circle, using the right hand. When each dribbler reaches starting position, they hand the balls to the players on the right.
3. Practice continues until everyone has dribbled and returned the balls to the five starters.
4. Players repeat the drill, dribbling in the opposite direction and using the left hand.

Pivot

Pivot, Pass, and Dribble (Figure 3.19)

1. Arrange six players in a file line with ten feet between each.
2. The starting player pivots, passes the ball to the next person, then takes the position of that player.
3. The player with the ball repeats this process until the last player receives the ball.
4. The last player dribbles back to the starting position.
5. Play continues in this manner until all participants return to their original positions.

FIGURE   3.19
Pivot, Pass, and Dribble.

FIGURE   3.20
Line Rebound.

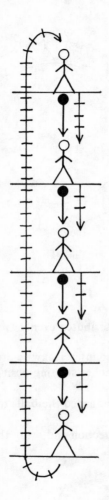

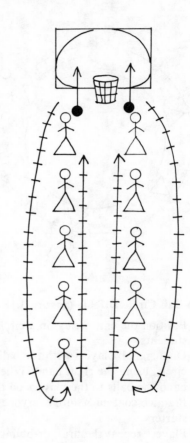

Shoot and Rebound

Line Rebound (Figure 3.20)

1. Players form two file lines on each side of the basket.
2. The first player in each line taps or tosses the ball against the backboard once and runs to the end of the line.
3. Each player in line repeats the process.

Five-Foot Shoot (Figure 3.21)

1. Assign approximately five players per basket. Use all available balls.
2. Each player shoots and rebounds own ball from a five-foot line, then makes two baskets before moving back to a ten-foot line.
3. The same procedure is followed at the ten-foot line and then at the foul line.
4. Players take turns in a set order and repeat routine a designated number of times.

Spot Shoot (Figure 3.22)

1. Players at each basket shoot and then rebound from each of eight designated floor spots.
2. Players must score a basket from each spot, beginning with number 1 in figure 3.22, before moving to the next consecutive number.
3. When a player misses a shot, the next player shoots, beginning on the spot where they missed on the previous turn.

FIGURE   3.21
Five-Foot Shoot.

FIGURE   3.22
Spot Shoot.

FIGURE   3.23
Variation on the Spot Shoot: School.

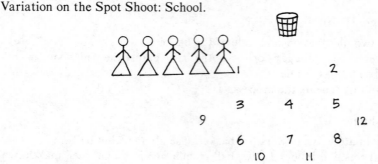

FIGURE   3.24
Triangle Shoot.

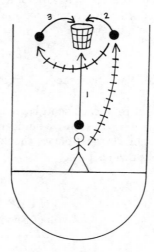

Variation

School (Figure 3.23): Choose twelve positions rather than eight. Players advance to the next number, or "grade," as they successfully complete each shot. The players completing all twelve shots "graduate" from "school."

Triangle Shoot (Figure 3.24)

1. Arrange players at the foul line in file formation.
2. The leader shoots from the foul line, rebounds the ball, shoots from the right, then shoots from the left side of the basket. (The type of shot is specified by the teacher.)
3. After completing all three shots, the shooter passes to the next player and goes to the end of the line.
4. This shooting sequence is performed by each player.

FIGURE   3.25
Continuous Shoot and Rebound.

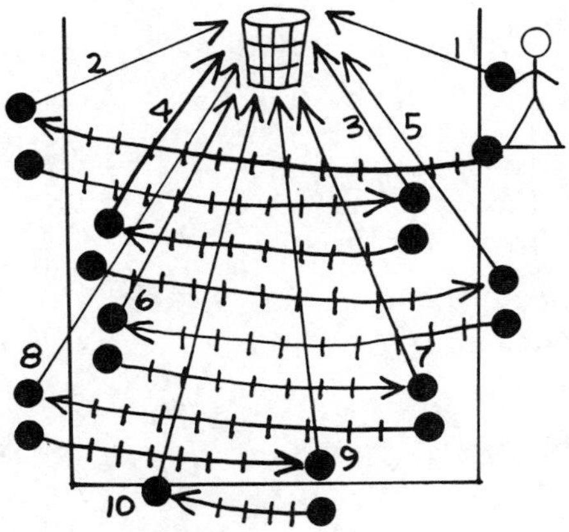

FIGURE   3.26
Partner Shot and Rebound.

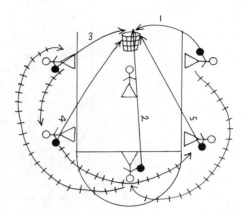

Continuous Shoot and Rebound (Figure 3.25)

1. The player with the ball begins shooting at baseline position from the right side of the basket (number 1 in figure 3.25).
2. The player rebounds the ball and shoots from the same position on the left side (number 2 in figure 3.25).
3. The player rebounds the ball again and shoots from position 3 and each position in order. (Mark each position or instruct students to move from right to left for each shot and back three feet for every other shot.)
4. Each player takes a total of ten shots. The final shot is made from the foul line.
5. Position players waiting to shoot under the basket.

Variation

Shoot from each position until a basket is made.

Partner Shot and Rebound (Figure 3.26)

1. Pair students. One player shoots and one player rebounds.
2. The shooter takes a shot from each numbered position in sequence, beginning with number 1 in figure 3.26. After each shot, the shooter moves to the next position.
3. The partner rebounds each shot from in front of the basket and then passes the ball to the shooter at each of the numbered positions.
4. After the ball has been shot from all five positions, partners reverse roles and continue play.

FIGURE   3.27
Foul Shot Practice.

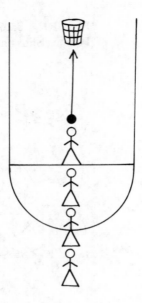

Foul Shot (Figure 3.27)

1. Players line up in file formation at the foul line.
2. The leader shoots a foul shot, rebounds the ball, and passes to the next player in line.
3. Players continue shooting until each player has scored, or until a designated number of points has been scored.

Dribble and Pass

Target Pass (Figure 3.28)

1. Arrange players in a file line, each player with a ball.
2. The first player dribbles to a passing line, passes against the wall a designated number of times, then dribbles to the back of the line.
3. The next person begins as the preceding player starts the return dribble.

Shuttle

1. Proceed as in figure 3.11.
2. Add a dribble before the pass.

Weave

1. Proceed as in figure 3.12.
2. Add a dribble before the pass.

FIGURE   3.28
Target Pass.

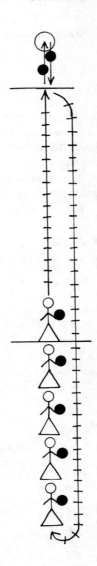

Pass and Shoot

Move It to Shoot (Figure 3.29)

1. Players, standing six feet apart, form a semicircle approximately six to eight feet from the basket.
2. The player on the far left begins by passing to the right. The pattern continues to the right until the ball reaches the last player, who shoots the ball.
3. The shooter rebounds the ball and moves to the far left position. The other players move one position to the right.
4. The new leader begins the passing sequence again.
5. Repeat the drill until all players are back in their original places.

Variation

Repeat the drill, commencing from the right side of the basket; or change the position of the semicircle so shots are taken from several positions.

Eight Pass (Figure 3.30)

1. Four players, standing three to four feet apart, form a semicircle six to eight feet from the basket, with the fifth player positioned under the basket.
2. The left outside player passes the ball to the player under the basket, who passes to the next player in line.
3. Passing continues in and out until the original player receives the eighth pass. This player shoots and rebounds while all other players move one position to the left.

FIGURE   3.29
Move It to Shoot.

FIGURE   3.30
Eight Pass.

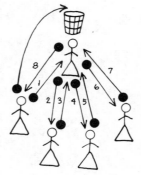

FIGURE   3.31
Lane Zigzag Pass.

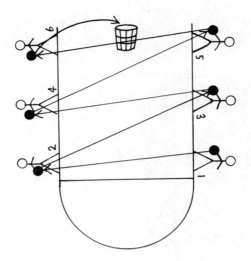

4. The shooter passes the ball to the left outside player and then moves under the basket.
5. Passing and shooting continues until players are back to their original places.

Variation

Beginning with any player in the semicircle, pass in and out until the eighth pass is received. This player shoots the ball.

Lane Zigzag Pass (Figure 3.31)

1. Players line up on the perimeters of the foul lane.
2. Players pass the ball back and forth across the lane in zigzag fashion from player number 1 to player number 6 (see figure 3.31).
3. Player number 6 shoots, rebounds the ball, and moves to position 1. All other players move in sequence to the next numbered position.
4. After all players have shot from position 6, they repeat the sequence using position 5 as the shooting position.
5. The pattern continues until players have shot the ball from all numbered positions. When the ball has started and been shot from position 1, the ball will have been passed ten times.

Variation

Use a variety of passes and shots.

FIGURE 3.32
Lane Rotation and Shoot.

FIGURE 3.33
Shoot and Move.

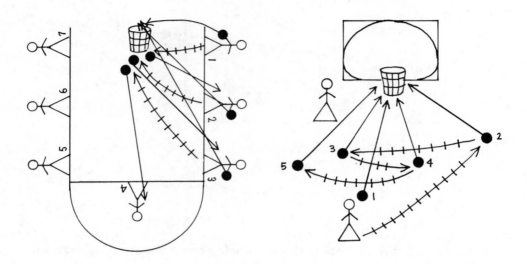

Lane Rotation and Shoot (Figure 3.32)

1. Six players stand on the perimeters of the foul lane; the seventh player stands on the foul line.
2. Beginning with player number 1 (see figure 3.32), each player shoots, rebounds, and passes to the next player in order.
3. After each player shoots, all players move to the right one position and then repeat the pattern.

Shoot and Move (Figure 3.33)

1. Two players work as a team: one is a shooter and one is a rebounder/passer.
2. The shooter releases the ball. The rebounder then rebounds the ball and passes to the shooter, who has moved to a position of choice to shoot the ball.
3. This action continues until the shooter has moved to five positions of choice.
4. The players exchange roles and play is repeated.

Lane Shoot and Move (Figure 3.34)

1. Three players form a team. One player is a shooter positioned on the lane. Two players, one on each side of the basket, are rebounders.
2. Play is initiated by the left rebounder, who passes to the shooter to shoot from position number 1 (figure 3.34).

FIGURE   3.34
Lane Shoot and Move.

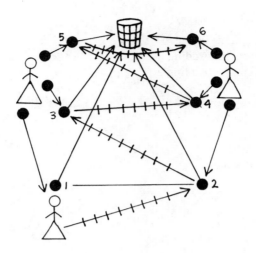

3. The right rebounder rebounds the shot. The shooter moves to position 2, taking the pass from the right rebounder. (After each shot, rebounders alternate retrieving the ball.)
4. This action continues until the shooter has moved to each numbered spot in sequence.
5. After the rebounder rebounds the ball from position 6, players rotate to the right.

Post Player Pass and Shoot (Figure 3.35)

1. Players form two file lines, twelve to fifteen feet apart, behind the foul line. Assign a permanent post player.
2. The post player passes the ball from the post to either of the advancing file line players. These players cross diagonally in front of the post player.
3. The player receiving the ball shoots (number 2 in figure 3.35a). The nonshooting player rebounds.
4. All line players complete this sequence.
5. When all players are proficient at the first sequence, add a pass (number 2 in figure 3.35b) to the other crossing player, who then becomes the shooter (number 3 in figure 3.35b).
6. All line players complete this sequence.
7. After players demonstrate proficiency at this drill, add another pass (number 3 in figure 3.35c) to the post player. The post player then shoots (4 in figure 3.35c), while the two line players cross the lane to rebound.

FIGURE 3.35
Post Player Pass and Shoot. (a) The
Simple Sequence. (b) Adding a Pass
Below the Basket. (c) Adding a
Second Pass.

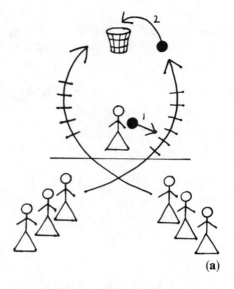

(a)

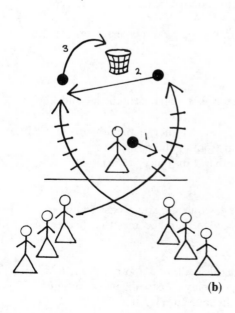

(b)

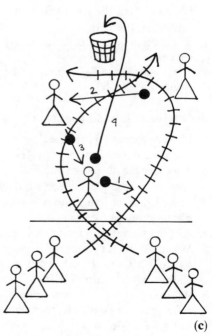

(c)

Dribble and Shoot

Shoot-Out (Figure 3.36)

1. Players are assigned to lines, one at each end of the court.
2. The first five players in each line have balls.
3. The first player in each line dribbles to the basket on the right and executes a lay-up shot.
4. The shooter rebounds and dribbles to midcourt. The next player in line begins the same procedure while the shooter continues on to the next basket for a lay-up.
5. This procedure continues until each player shoots and rebounds at each basket.
6. The ball is dribbled to the starting line and handed to the next player.

FIGURE   3.36
Shoot-Out.

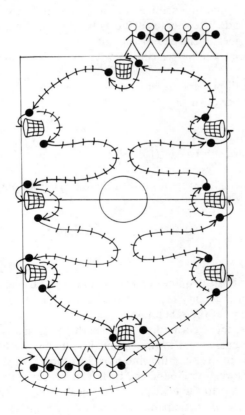

Variations

1. Repeat play in the opposite direction using left-handed lay-ups.
2. Position additional teams at other baskets with one ball per basket. The player with the ball dribbles the entire route, passing off to the next player, who repeats the process. The dribble to midcourt is eliminated. This variation is useful when your class contains more players and/or limited equipment. Take care that players do not travel or fail to execute the lay-up properly.
3. Substitute different shooting positions and types of shots (for example, use a jump shot).

Shoot Until You Make It (Figure 3.37)

1. Position players in four lines at midcourt (or in two lines at each basket). Two lines will shoot at one basket and two lines at the opposite basket.
2. The first player in each line dribbles to the basket and shoots from any position.
3. If the basket is made, the shooter dribbles back to the line, gives the ball to the next person, and goes to the end of the line.
4. If the shot is missed, the player continues to shoot, from any position, until a basket is scored.
5. Play continues until players return to their original positions or until each takes a designated number of turns.

Variations

1. Add a third line at each basket (for large classes or additional practice under pressure).
2. Rotate line position so players approach the basket from both sides.

Dribble, Pass, and Shoot

Lay-up (Figure 3.38)

1. Six to ten players form two lines on either side of the basket, with each line approximately ten to twenty feet from the basket. One line is the shooting line, and the other line does the rebounding.
2. The first player on the shooting line dribbles the ball, shoots the lay-up, and moves behind the basket and to the end of the rebounding line.
3. As the first player in the shooting line moves to shoot, the first player in the rebounding line moves to rebound the ball. This player then dribbles the ball a few feet and passes it to the next player in the shooting line.
4. Play continues until all participants have taken a designated number of shots or have returned to original position.

FIGURE   3.37
Shoot Until You Make It.

FIGURE   3.38
Practicing the Lay-up.

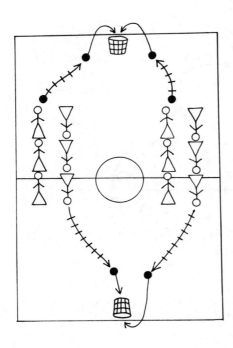

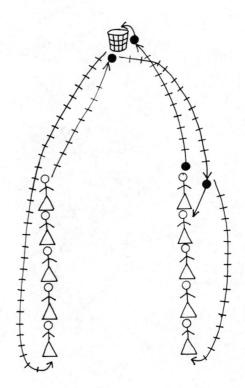

Variations

1. Follow the same procedure shooting from the opposite side of the basket or from the middle of the court.
2. Every player in the shooting line has a ball. After the shot, the rebounder keeps the ball and dribbles to the opposite end of the court to shoot a lay-up. This player then rebounds the ball and dribbles it back to the end of the shooting line.

FIGURE   3.39
Russian Lay-up.

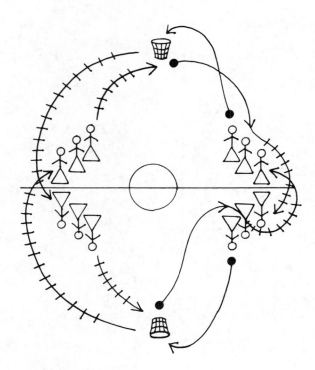

Russian Lay-up (Figure 3.39)

1. Players form shooting and rebounding lines on each end of the court. Each line should be twenty to thirty feet from the basket. The last players stand on the center line. Both shooting lines are positioned on one side of the court with the rebounding lines on the opposite side.
2. The first player in each shooting line dribbles forward, shoots the lay-up, and moves behind the basket to the end of the rebounding line on the opposite end of the court.
3. The first player in each rebounding line moves at the same time the shooter moves. The rebounding player rebounds the ball and dribbles to the end of the shooting line at the opposite end of the court.
4. Play continues for a specified time period or until a designated number of baskets has been scored.

FIGURE   3.40
Four-Player Full Court Movement.

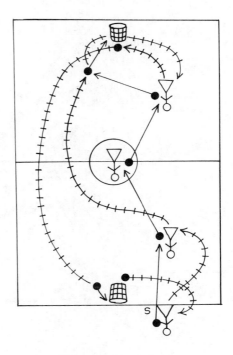

Four-Player Full Court Movement (Figure 3.40)

1. Four players station themselves on the court, one at each quarter-court, one at midcourt (in the center circle), and one behind the endline.
2. The player behind the endline initiates play, throwing the ball to the player standing in the closest quarter-court. The endline player then assumes the quarter-court position.
3. The quarter-court player passes to the player at midcourt and moves to a position on the left side of the opposite basket.
4. The player at midcourt passes to the player in the other quarter-court position.
5. The quarter-court player passes to the player who has moved into position to the left of the basket.
6. This player shoots the ball and then takes the quarter-court position to the right of the basket. The quarter-court player who was to the right of the basket rebounds the ball, dribbles to the opposite end of the court, and executes a lay-up.
7. The shooting player rebounds his or her own ball and moves behind the endline to begin the drill again.
8. The midcourt player does not move until new positions are assigned.

FIGURE 3.41
Around-the-Court Cut and Pass.

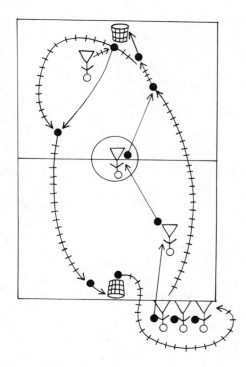

Around-the-Court Cut and Pass (Figure 3.41)

1. Three to five players, each with a ball, position themselves on the baseline. Three additional stand at quarter-court, midcourt (in the center circle), and to the left side of the opposite basket.
2. The first player on the baseline passes to the quarter-court player and runs to the opposite end of the court, ready to receive a pass on the right side of the basket.
3. The quarter-court player passes to the midcourt player, who passes to the original baseline player now positioned to the right of the basket.
4. This player shoots the ball and moves to the left side of the court toward the center line.
5. The player to the left of the basket recovers the ball and passes it to the shooter, who is now positioned close to the center line. This player dribbles to the starting end of the court to shoot and rebound a lay-up and then moves to the end of the starting line.
6. Players rotate positions after all baseline players have followed this pattern.

Variations

1. Vary the types of shots practiced.
2. Require players to shoot until they make a basket.

FIGURE   3.42
Two-Team Full Court Movement.

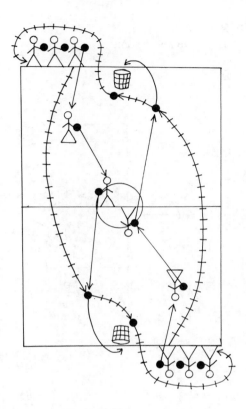

Two-Team Full Court Movement (Figure 3.42)

1. Assign five players to each half-court, three behind each baseline at opposite corners, one at each quarter-court, and one from each team at midcourt.
2. Conduct the drill simultaneously on both sides of the court.
3. On each team, the first baseline player passes to the nearest quarter-court player and moves to a position close to the basket at the opposite end of the court.
4. The quarter-court player on each side passes to the midcourt player on the same team.
5. Each midcourt player passes to the original baseline player who has moved to the opposite basket.
6. Each baseline player shoots, rebounds, and moves to the end of the line behind the other baseline players.
7. Play continues until all players are back to their original places.
8. The quarter-court and midcourt players rotate with the baseline players and play begins again.

FIGURE   3.43
Ten-Pass Move and Shoot.

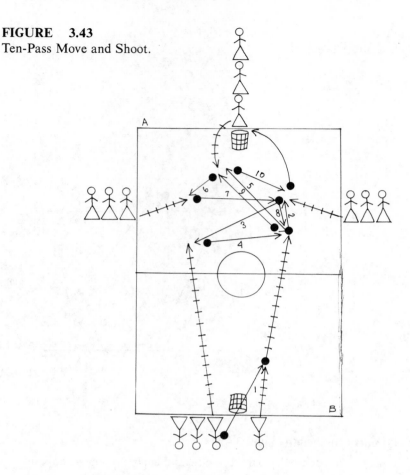

Ten-Pass Move and Shoot (Figure 3.43)

1. Position three to four players under each full court basket and behind each quarter-court sideline in one half-court (see figure 3.43). The players behind endline *A* are "centers." The players at quarter-court are "forwards." The players at endline *B* are "guards."
2. The first two guards initiate the play.
3. One guard moves to quarter-court. The player with the ball passes to the quarter-court guard. This guard then dribbles the ball beyond the center line.
4. The guard who just passed the ball moves across the center line on the opposite side of the court.
5. The first forward and center in each line move onto the court near the free throw lane.
6. Five players are now in position to pass the ball. Players may pass to any of the five.

FIGURE   3.44
Six-Player Pass and Shoot.

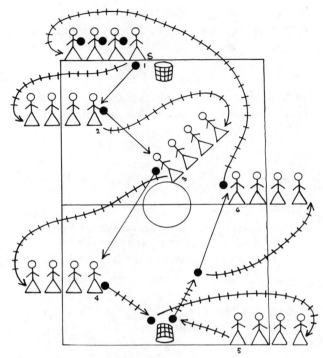

7. Players must make ten passes. The player receiving the tenth pass shoots the ball.
8. If this player misses the shot, any player may rebound the ball. Players then repeat the ten-pass process.
9. When one team of five players makes a basket, these players rotate one line clockwise. (If the instructor prefers to have students practice specific positions, players may return to the same lines.)

Variations

1. Each time the pass pattern starts again, reduce the number of passes by one until only one pass is required before a player shoots.
2. Add a short dribble before each pass.

Six-Player Pass and Shoot (Figure 3.44)

1. Arrange lines of four to five players at six positions on the court (see figure 3.44). Each player in the starting position (S) has a ball.
2. The first players in lines 1, 2, and 3 pass to the first player in the next line and go to the end of that line.
3. The first player in line 4, after receiving the ball, dribbles, shoots, and goes to the end of line 5.
4. The first player in line 5 rebounds, dribbles away from the basket, passes to the first player in line 6 and goes to the end of that line.

5. The first player in line 6 dribbles to the end of line 1.
6. As the first player in line 4 receives the ball, the second player in line 1 begins the same pattern.

Variation

The first player in line 6 receives the ball, dribbles to the basket close to line 1, and executes a designated type of shot. The shooter rebounds the ball and goes to the end of line 1.

Court Play

Jump Ball (Figure 3.45)

1. Ten players position themselves around the center circle or key, as in a game.
2. Two players are designated as jumpers. A leader or teacher is the tosser.
3. The tosser specifies where the ball is to be directed when tapped.

FIGURE   3.45
Practicing the Jump Ball.

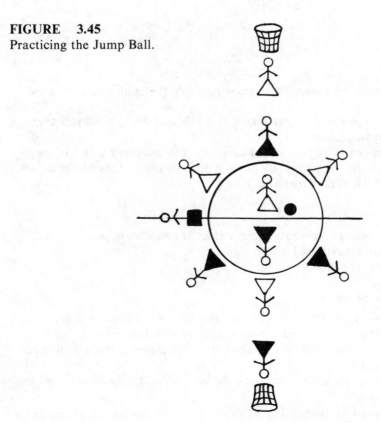

4. After five taps, the jumpers exchange places with other players positioned around the circle.
5. The practice is repeated until all players have been jumpers and achieved some proficiency.

Variation

After the tap, the ball is quickly passed to the player near the basket, who shoots, rebounds, and passes the ball to the tosser.

Offensive Tactics (Figure 3.46a-l)

1. Five players position themselves around the key.
2. The ball is passed sharply and accurately to each player.
3. After the ball is returned to the first player, the teacher selects one of the following patterns for the students to execute:

FIGURE   3.46
Practicing Offensive Tactics: Twelve Different Passing Patterns. (a)–(f) Passing to One Side of the Key. (g)–(l) Passing to the Opposite Side.

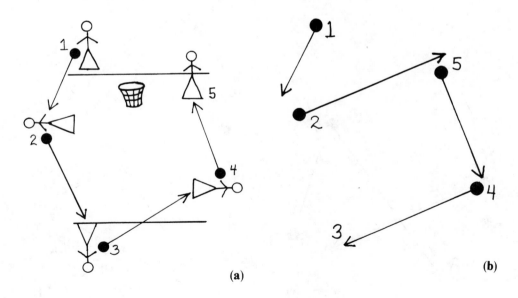

(a)   (b)

FIGURE   3.46—*Continued*

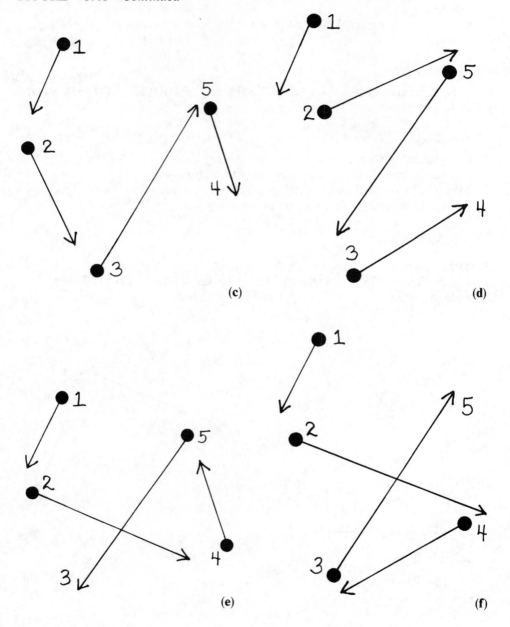

4. Players repeat the pattern to the opposite side of the key.

FIGURE   3.46—*Continued*

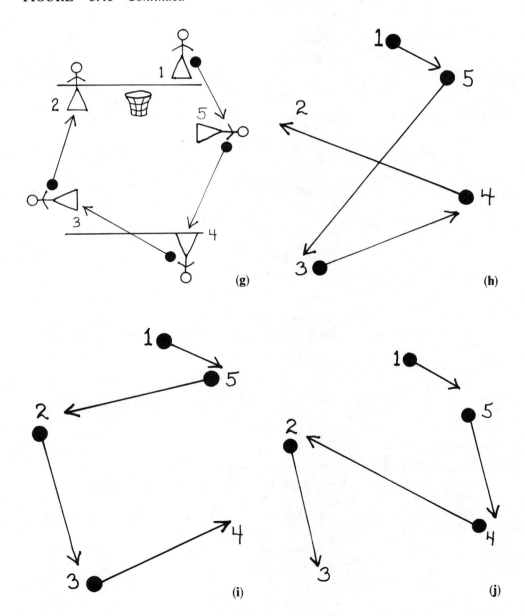

(g)

(h)

(i)

(j)

FIGURE   **3.46**—*Continued*

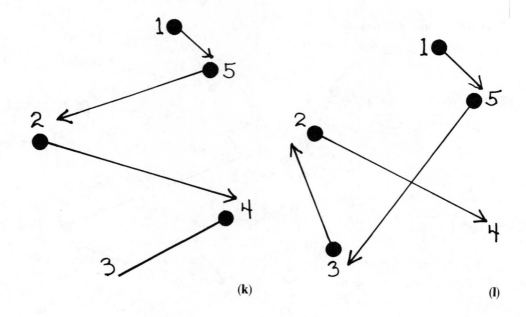

(k)   (l)

5. Players shift one position counterclockwise and the drills begin again.
6. Students repeat the patterns until each player has the opportunity to play each position.

Variation

The last player to receive the ball in each pattern shoots, and the first player rebounds the ball.

Defensive Tactics

1. Using the drills diagrammed in figure 3.46, assign defensive players to appropriate positions. These players try to intercept the ball as the offensive players pass.
2. Assign defensive players, when appropriate, to any of the other drills described in this chapter.

LEAD-UP GAMES

Ten Pass (Grades 5–12)

Equipment

Basketballs, vests or pinnies

Procedures

1. Assign teams of five players to designated areas of the gym determined by the number of students that must be accommodated.
2. The offensive team attempts to score a point by completing ten consecutive passes between team members.
3. The defensive team tries to intercept the ball.
4. Each time an interception occurs or a point is scored, the offensive and defensive teams reverse positions.
5. Play continues until one team scores ten points.

Basketball Keep-Away (Grades 5–12)

Equipment

Basketballs, vests or pinnies

Procedures

1. An area defined by marked lines, such as the free throw lane or free throw circle, is designated as a playing area.
2. Each participant within the designated playing area has a ball.
3. On a signal, each player begins dribbling with one hand, using the other hand to hit opponents' balls away. A player whose ball is knocked away is eliminated from play. The object is to be the last player still dribbling.
4. The last player dribbling is declared winner.
5. Several games can go on at once in different areas of the court.
6. Eliminated players go to a designated area and start another game.

Basket Race Ball (Grades 5–12)

Equipment

Basketballs, vests or pinnies, four bases

Procedures (Figure 3.47)

1. Arrange four bases as shown in figure 3.47, allowing adequate space for players to go around the bases and overrun home base.

FIGURE   3.47
Basket Race Ball.

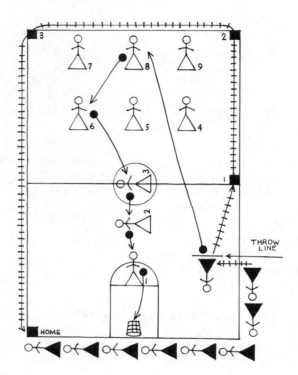

2. Divide the class into teams of approximately ten players each.
3. The player on the throwing line runs within the court and throws the basketball over the center line. This player then runs to touch first, second, third, and home base.
4. A fielder catches or recovers the ball and throws to another fielder.
5. The receiving fielder must then pass the ball to player number 3 at center court, who passes ahead to number 2, who in turn passes to player number 1 standing at the free throw line. Player number 1 shoots the ball from the foul line. If player 1 makes a basket before the runner crosses home base, the runner is out.
6. If the shooter misses, successive shots may be taken from wherever the ball is rebounded. If the ball is retrieved under the basket, the player may take three dribbles to get into a better position.
7. If the base runner crosses home base before the shooter can make a basket, the runner's team scores a point.
8. The players on the fielding team move up one position after each out or point. When all players on the throwing team have completed one turn, the teams switch positions.

FIGURE 3.48
Sideline Basketball.

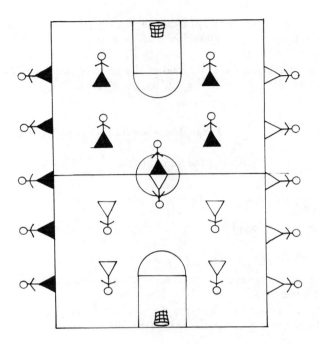

9. The following violations by the fielding team result in a point for the throwing team: traveling, failing to make at least one pass to another fielder before passing to player number 3, failing to pass the ball from player number 3, to 2, to 1.
10. The following violations by the throwing team result in an out: failure to throw the ball across the center line so it lands in the court (allow two tries) or failure to touch base when running.

Sideline Basketball (Grades 5–12)

Equipment

Basketball, vests or pinnies, basketball hoops

Procedures (Figure 3.48)

1. Divide the class into two teams. Five players from each team are the court players and play regulation basketball, with one change in the rules: they are allowed to pass to fellow team members behind the sidelines to move the ball down court.
2. The remaining players stand on the sidelines (one team on each side of the court) to catch the ball and pass it back to the court players.

3. Sideline players may not shoot the ball or cross the sideline. They may pass only to court players, not to other sideline players.
4. At the end of the designated playing time, or after each basket is scored, the court players move to the end of the line at the sideline and five new players move from the sideline to replace them on the court.

Team Hand-Basket Ball (Grades 9–12)

This game is a modification of team handball adapted so that only basketball skills are used.

Equipment
Basketball, vests or pinnies, basketball hoops

Procedures (Figure 3.49)
1. The game is played by two teams of seven players each: six rovers and a rebounder.
2. Rebounders are the only players allowed in the goal areas.
3. Rovers dribble and pass the ball down court, then shoot from outside the goal area line.

FIGURE   3.49
Team Hand-Basket Ball Court.

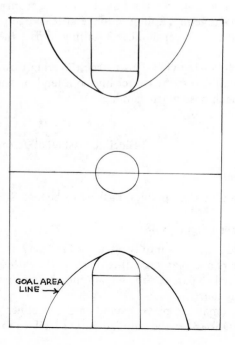

GOAL AREA
LINE →

4. The goal area is marked at a distance from the basket to challenge the players. (Advanced players may have a goal area far from the basket.)
5. When one team commits a violation, such as an illegal dribble or holding the ball longer than three seconds, the other team gains possession of the ball at the point of the violation.
6. Rovers who move across the goal area line also commit a violation. In this situation, the other team gets a free pass from anywhere on the line marking the goal area.
7. The game begins with a jump ball at the center line. After one team scores a goal, the other team puts the ball in play at the center line with a free pass.
8. If a foul is committed, the player fouled takes one free throw and the ball is then put back in play at the center line by the shooting player.
9. Play continues when a shot is missed.
10. A goal counts two points.

Variations

1. Rotate players in from the sideline every five minutes.
2. Additional players line up along each sideline to receive passes from teammates on the court and help move the ball down court (see the previous description of Sideline Basketball). Sideline players may not hold the ball longer than three seconds, dribble, or travel with the ball.

SKILL TESTS

Timed Bank Shots

Each player shoots from either side of the basket, recovers the ball, and shoots again. Count the number of baskets made in thirty seconds.

Variation

Players take their first shots from the free throw line.

Wall Pass (Figure 3.50)

Each player begins in floor zone *A* and throws the ball diagonally to zone *A* on the wall (see figure 3.50). After throwing the ball, the player runs to zone *B* to retrieve the ball, then throws it diagonally to the corresponding zone (*B*) on the wall. It is illegal to throw the ball from the neutral area between the zones, and it is illegal for the ball to land on the wall in the neutral area between zones. Score all the legal passes the player makes in thirty seconds. Allow each player three trials.

Obstacle Dribble (Figure 3.51)

On the command "go," each player dribbles legally around cones (or other obstacles) and back to the starting line. A fumbled ball must be brought back to the starting line, where the dribbler begins again. Score the time it takes the player to complete the obstacle course. Give each student three trials dribbling with the right hand, and three dribbling with the left hand.

FIGURE   3.50
Wall Pass.

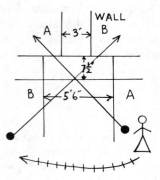

FIGURE   3.51
Obstacle Dribble.

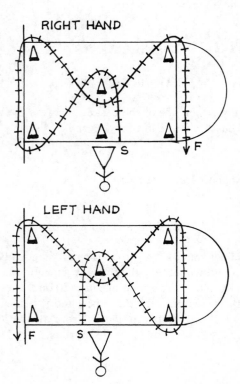

Free Throws

The participant shoots five or ten free throws. Record the number of successful shots the player makes. Give each shooter three trials.

Spot Shoot (Figure 3.52)

Designate five shooting areas around the basket. The participant shoots one time from each spot. Score the number of successful shots the player makes. Give each shooter three trials.

FIGURE   3.52
Spot Shoot.

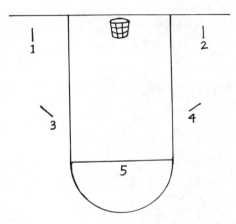

WRITTEN TEST

MATCHING BASKETBALL TERMS   **Note:** Some answers appear more than once, others not at all.

a. zone
b. violation
c. two
d. traveling
e. throw-in
f. three
g. one
h. man-to-man
i. free throw
j. foul
k. five
l. double dribble
m. guarding
n. charging
o. blocking

_____   1. Moving into an opponent while you are handling the ball
_____   2. The number of players on a team
_____   3. Dribbling the ball with both hands

_____ 4. The number of points scored for a free throw
_____ 5. Putting the ball in play from the sideline
_____ 6. Moving the ball illegally
_____ 7. An infraction for which the opposing team is awarded one or more free throws
_____ 8. An infraction for which the opposing team is awarded a throw-in
_____ 9. Impeding the progress of an opponent by personal contact
_____ 10. The number of points scored for a field goal
_____ 11. A system of defense that covers areas of the court
_____ 12. The number of seconds an offensive player may stand in the key before having to move
_____ 13. Taking more than two steps while in possession of the ball
_____ 14. An unguarded shot awarded for a foul
_____ 15. A system of defense that involves guarding individually assigned opponents

IDENTIFICATION Mark whether each of the following situations or skills is legal (L), a violation (V), or a foul (F).

_____ 16. Charging
_____ 17. Pivoting
_____ 18. Using three guards
_____ 19. Double dribbling
_____ 20. Performing a bounce pass
_____ 21. Traveling
_____ 22. Offense in lane for three seconds
_____ 23. Blocking
_____ 24. Dribbling
_____ 25. Substitution

DIAGRAM Diagram and label the areas of the court.

TEST KEY

1. n	6. b	11. a	16. F	21. V
2. k	7. j	12. f	17. L	22. L
3. b	8. b	13. d	18. L	23. F
4. g	9. o	14. i	19. V	24. L
5. e	10. c	15. h	20. L	25. L

CHAPTER FOUR

FLAG FOOTBALL

Popularized in the United States, football now rivals baseball as both a participation and spectator sport. Flag football provides the opportunity for players at all skill levels to participate in a less hazardous game than regulation football. It can be a gender-free sport played by teams with as few as four players and as many as nine.

EQUIPMENT

Footballs: Regulation, Junior, Nerf
Rip flags and belts
Cones or field markers
Targets

SUGGESTIONS FOR INSTRUCTIONAL PROFICIENCY

1. If possible, provide one ball for every two people, or at least one for every four people.
2. Substitute a Nerf ball or junior-sized football when instructing small and inexperienced players.
3. Stress safety and organize practices to avoid collisions. Flag football, by definition, should be played as a noncontact sport.
4. Teach students to catch the ball with outstretched arms and then cradle it against the body so the pointed ends do not cause injury.
5. Integrate rules, strategies, and specialized vocabulary as you teach basic skills. This permits students to become knowledgeable spectators as well as players.
6. Establish a line of direction and conduct practices so students face away from the sun.
7. Organize the class so errors can be easily observed and corrected.
8. Reduce or modify playing fields for elementary school participants or other beginners.
9. Provide opportunities for students to learn and play all positions.
10. Use coed game rules that include both sexes in each play and protect players from unsafe conditions.
11. Practice flag-pulling techniques with an emphasis on safety and fair play.

TEACHING THE BASICS

The following progression is suggested:

1. **Pass and Catch:** Teach both skills together whenever possible as both are fundamental to game success. Students should develop proficiency in these two areas before moving on to the next skills.

   Forward spiral pass
   Lateral pass

2. **Hike (center):** Develop skill in centering or hiking the ball to a backfield player five yards away.
3. **Kick:** Select the type of kick according to player experience.

   Punt
   Place kick

4. **Game Situations:** Students should practice passing and catching as well as the following skills and techniques:

   Run, sidestep
   Handoff
   Carry
   Pitchout
   Leader techniques (quarterback)
   Flag pull
   Offensive stances (three-point, semicrouch)
   Defensive stance (semicrouch)
   Rules and terminology (including penalties)

5. **Strategy:** Teach strategies and plays to give students a basis for creating their own game tactics.

   Offensive tactics
       Short yardage plays
       Long yardage plays
       Quick kick
   Defensive tactics
       Man-to-man coverage
       Zone coverage
       Punt coverage
   Kickoff

DRILLS

Pass and Catch

Partner Pass and Catch (Figure 4.1)

1. Partners face each other, standing approximately fifteen to twenty feet apart.
2. Students pass the ball back and forth.
3. Vary practice by passing the ball in the following ways:

     High
     Low
     Right
     Left
     Over the head
     Short

FIGURE   4.1
Partner Pass and Catch.

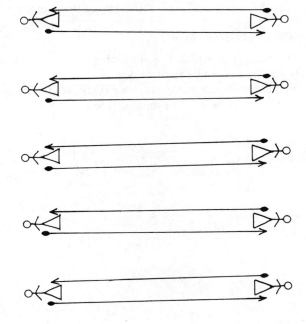

FIGURE   4.2
Variation on the Partner
Pass and Catch.

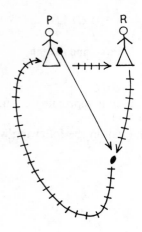

Variation (Figure 4.2)

Partners stand side by side. One player prepares to pass to the other. The receiver runs out to catch the pass and then runs back to the starting point. Players reverse roles.

Seven Pass and Catch (Figure 4.3)

1. Players form groups of five. In each group, four passers stand side by side facing a receiver fifteen feet away.
2. The receiver attempts to catch a pass from each player in turn, beginning with the passer farthest to the receiver's left.

FIGURE   4.3
Seven Pass and Catch.

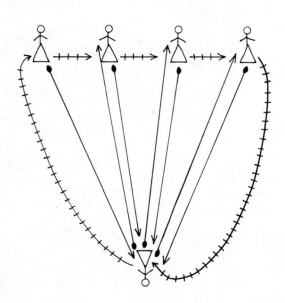

3. After each reception, the receiver passes the ball to the next passer.
4. The first pass is thrown high, the second low, the third to the left, and the next to the right.
5. After catching the last pass, the receiver returns with the ball to the far left position. All other players move one place to their left.
6. Continue until players return to original positions.

File Pass and Catch (Figure 4.4)

1. Arrange players in a file line at ten-yard intervals.
2. The first player passes the ball to the second player.
3. Each successive player passes the ball to the next player until the ball reaches the end of the file line.
4. The last player turns with the ball, and begins the same passing-and-catching sequence in reverse direction. The pattern continues until players pass the ball back to starting position.
5. Players repeat the entire sequence four times.

Variation (Figure 4.5)

The ball is passed to the end of the file line as described. The last player then runs with the ball to the front of the line and all players move back ten yards. Play is complete when all players return to original positions.

FIGURE   4.4
File Pass and Catch.

FIGURE   4.5
Variation on the File Pass and Catch.

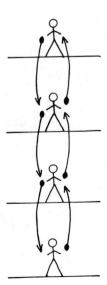

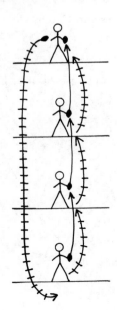

Triangle Pass and Catch (Figure 4.6)

1. Students form groups of three. Each group forms a triangle with players approximately ten yards apart.
2. One person acts as passer. The two receivers stand at the other points of the triangle, facing away from the passer.
3. The passer signals "turn," and at the same time throws the ball to either of the receivers as they turn to face the oncoming ball.
4. The receiver carries the ball to the passing position and the other two players rotate to occupy the remaining points.

Triangle Screen Pass and Catch (Figure 4.7)

1. Players form groups of three. Each group forms a triangle with players approximately ten yards apart.
2. Player number 1 acts as quarterback, player 2 as the receiver, and player 3 as the screen.
3. Player 1 signals player 2 to begin running toward player 3.
4. At the same time, player 3 runs in front of 2. Player 3 waves the hands up high to obstruct 2's view of the ball.
5. Player 1 throws the ball to 2 as 2 and 3 pass each other.
6. Players rotate positions. (Player 2 now becomes the quarterback, 3 becomes the receiver, and 1 becomes the screen.)
7. Players continue to rotate positions after each play.

FIGURE   4.6
Triangle Pass and Catch.

FIGURE   4.7
Triangle Screen Pass and Catch.

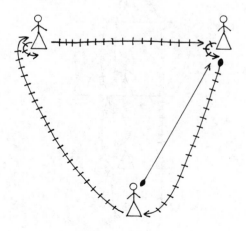

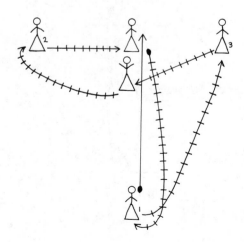

Team Pass and Catch (Figure 4.8)

1. Receivers form file lines approximately five feet behind two passers.
2. On a signal, the first receiver in each file line moves forward. As they reach the space between the two passers, each receiver crosses to the other side of the field.
3. Each receiver runs to a spot at least ten feet in front of the opposite passer to receive the ball from that passer.
4. After catching the ball, each receiver continues to run around a cone and back to take the position of the passer.
5. The passers each move to the end of their own file line and play begins again.
6. The drill ends when players return to their original places.

FIGURE   4.8
Team Pass and Catch.

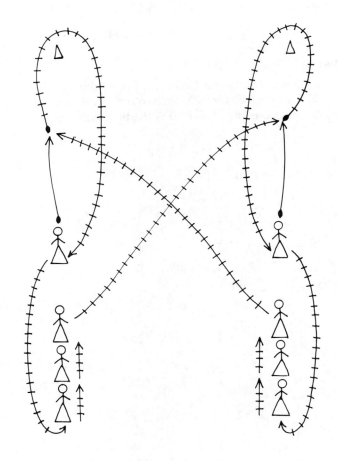

Pass Patterns (Figure 4.9)

  1. Pairs of students practice specific pass patterns.
     a. Square Out
     b. Crossing Pattern
     c. Hook In
     d. Hook Out
     e. Streak
     f. Post-Cross
     g. Corner
     h. Post
     i. Out and Up
  2. Rotate passing and catching positions unless players are developing specialized skills.

Hike

Hike Ball (Figure 4.10)

  1. Arrange players in a file line at five-yard intervals.
  2. The first player hikes the ball to the second player.
  3. Each succeeding player hikes the ball until it reaches the end of the file.

FIGURE   4.9
Nine Different Pass Patterns.

FIGURE   4.10
Hike Ball.

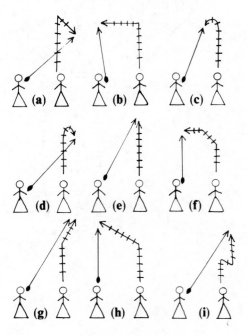

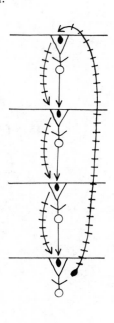

4. The last player runs with the ball to the front of the line and all players move back five yards.
5. The drill is complete when players are back in their original positions.

Hike, Run, and Catch (Figure 4.11)

1. Arrange players five yards apart in file lines.
2. The first player in each line hikes the ball to the second player, then runs downfield approximately ten yards and turns to receive the forward pass.
3. The receiver then throws the ball back to the passer and runs to the end of the line.
4. All other players move forward one position.
5. Repeat the pattern until all players are back in their original positions.

Variation

Play for accuracy. Score one point for each pass completed over a given line. (Distance to the line depends upon players' skill). Each player takes two turns.

FIGURE   4.11
Hike, Run, and Catch.

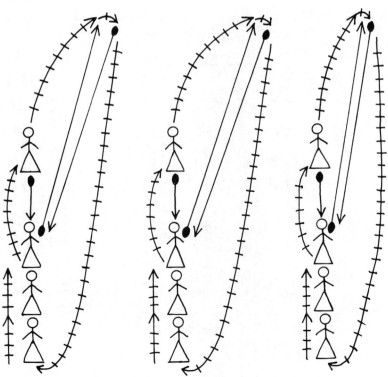

Kick (Punt)

One-Line Kick (Punt) (Figure 4.12)

1. Position players side by side in one line, six to eight feet apart. Each player has a ball.
2. On a signal, players kick the balls.
3. On another signal, players run to retrieve the balls.
4. Players form a new kicking line on the opposite side of the playing area to kick back to the original line.

Partner Kick (Punt) (Figure 4.13)

1. Partners face each other, standing approximately twenty to thirty feet apart.
2. Students kick the ball back and forth.

Variation

Each time a player catches the ball counts one point. At the end of a specified time, the player or team with the highest number of points is declared the winner.

FIGURE   4.12
One-Line Kick (Punt).

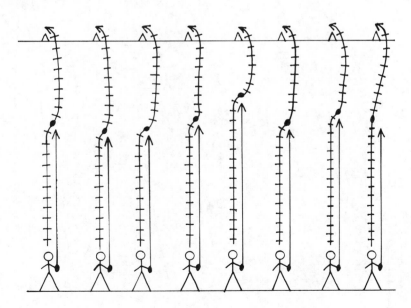

FIGURE   4.13
Partner Kick (Punt).

FIGURE   4.14
Kicking for Distance.

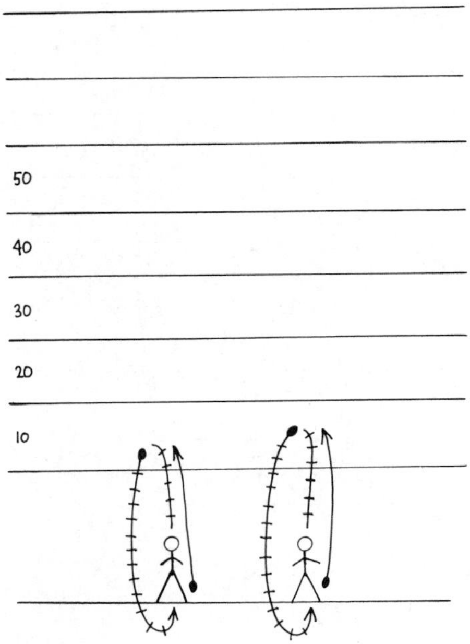

50

40

30

20

10

Accuracy and Distance Kick

Set up as many target areas as space and equipment allow for the following drills.

1. (Figure 4.14) Mark the field at ten-yard intervals beginning twenty yards from the kicking line. (Call the first line the 10 yard line.) The first kick must land between the 10 and 20 yard lines. The second kick must land between the 20 and 30 yard lines. Repeat the procedure for each successive area.

2. (Figure 4.15) Place hula hoops approximately ten feet apart from one another in a target area thirty yards from players. Each player attempts to kick the ball so that it lands in the hoop directly ahead. When students gain proficiency, remove half of the hoops and kick the balls to a more challenging target. (If space is limited, partners stationed at either end of the target area may retrieve the balls and kick back.)

FIGURE   4.15
Kicking into Hula Hoops
for Distance and
Accuracy.

FIGURE   4.16
Kicking to Target Areas
to Gain Points for
Distance and Accuracy.

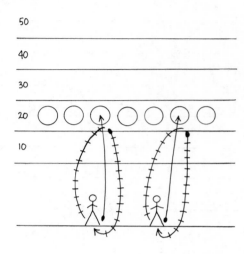

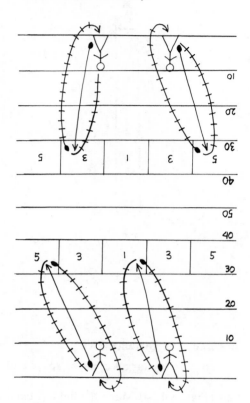

3. (Figure 4.16) Kick the ball into target areas assigned various points. Arrange scoring areas with lesser values in the middle of the field. Players attempt to score as many points as they can.

Kick (Place Kick)

Triad Place Kick (Figure 4.17)

1. Divide class into groups of three. In each group, one player holds the football, one place kicks the ball, and the third retrieves the ball.
2. The kicker place kicks the ball five times.
3. Players rotate and the action is repeated.

FIGURE   4.17
Triad Place Kick.

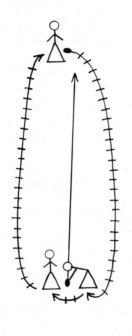

FIGURE   4.18
Run the Square.

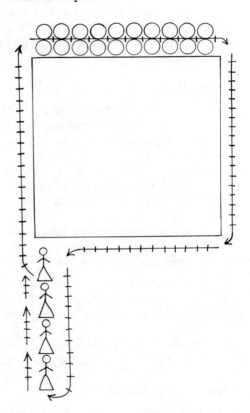

Accuracy and Distance Kick

Players place kick the ball, using the accuracy and distance drills previously described for punting.

Field Play: Running

Run the Square (Figure 4.18)

1. Place cones to mark an area ten yards square.
2. Players perform a different foot pattern on each side of the square:
   a. On the first side, players sprint.
   b. On the second side, players run through tires or hoops.

    c. On the third side, players run the grapevine.
    d. On the fourth side, players run backwards.
3. A new runner starts when the preceding runner begins the third side.
4. Each runner, after completing the square, returns to the end of the line. When all players return to their original positions, runners begin again in the opposite direction.

Sideline Run

1. Players form file lines along the sideline at ten-yard intervals. (The markings of a regulation football field may be used.)
2. The first players in each line run the width of the field or some other designated distance.
3. The next person in each line starts when the preceding player reaches midfield.
4. After all players reach the other side of the field, a new file line is formed and players return over the same route.
5. Players should practice various running steps: high knees, cross-over, grapevine, overstride, plant and cut, backwards, hoop or tire run.

Figure Eight Run (Figure 4.19)

1. Arrange four cones five yards apart from one another.
2. Players form a file line five yards in front of the first cone.
3. The first player runs in a zigzag between cones, returning to the front of the line.
4. The first player hands the ball off to the next player, who repeats the action.
5. Play continues until each player is back to original position.

Variation (Figure 4.20)

Substitute players for cones. The runner completes the course, hands off to the next person in the file line, and returns to take the distant player position. Each stationary player then runs forward one position. The front player goes to the end of the file line and the next player begins the course.

Follow-the-Leader (Foot Movement)

1. The leader stands in front of the group and motions directions for runners' movement (forward, back, right, left).
2. Leader calls out specific foot patterns (for example, sidestep or grapevine) while directing movement.

FIGURE   4.19
Figure Eight Run.

FIGURE   4.20
Variation on the Figure Eight Run.

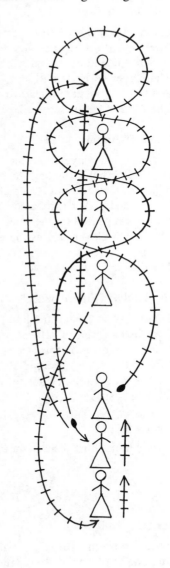

Field Play: Handoff, Pitchout, or Carry

Handoff Shuttle (Figure 4.21)

1. Players form shuttle lines opposite one another, one ball per shuttle.
2. The player with the ball moves forward to hand off to the oncoming player, then runs to the end of that player's line.
3. The player with the ball now hands off to the next person in the oncoming line and runs to the end of that line to begin play again.
4. The pattern continues until all players return to original positions.

File Handoff (Figure 4.22)

1. Arrange four players in a file line five yards apart from one another.
2. One player holds the ball, facing the remaining players. The player with the ball runs forward and hands off to the second player.
3. The second player turns and runs to hand off to the third player. The same action is repeated by the third player.
4. The fourth player carries the ball back to the start and players move back one position.
5. The drill ends when players return to their original positions.

Double Handoff (Figure 4.23)

1. Three players form a file line ten yards apart from one another.
2. The player with the ball carries it to the stationary center player, hands off, and runs forward to the third position.
3. After the first player completes the first handoff, the player from the third position runs to the center to receive the second handoff, then runs to the starting position to begin the drill again.

Variation

The player in the third position moves wide and receives a pitchout instead of a handoff.

Field Play: Flag Pulling

Partner Flag Pull

1. Players work in pairs. Each pair stands about ten yards apart, facing each other. One line of players is designated offense and the other defense.
2. On a signal, the offensive players run toward their defensive partners, who attempt to pull one or both flags.
3. Replace the flags and reverse roles.

FIGURE   4.21
Handoff Shuttle.

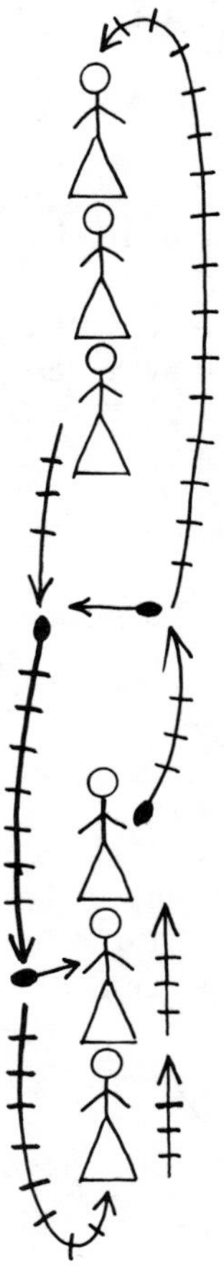

FIGURE   4.22
File Handoff.

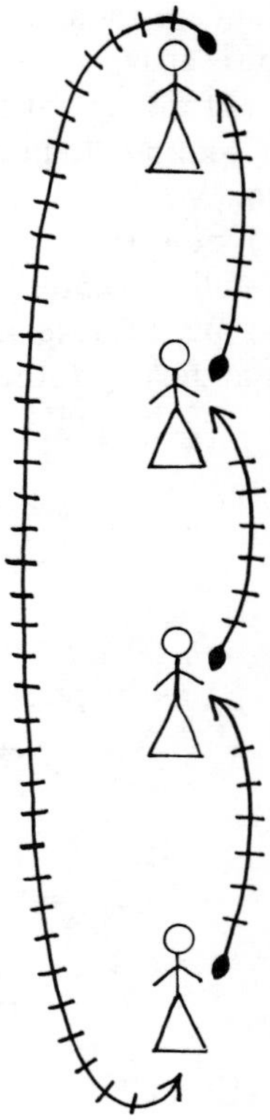

FIGURE   4.23
Double Handoff.

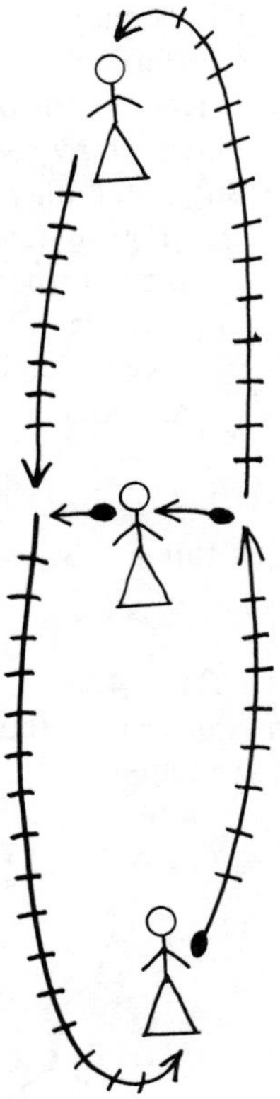

Variation

Offensive players make a half or whole turn to avoid the pull.

Team Flag Pull

1. Teams line up facing each other, approximately twenty-five yards apart.
2. On a signal, both teams run forward and attempt to pull the flags of the opposing team while protecting their own flags.
3. On another signal, play stops. The team with the most flags in their possession is the winner.

Field Play: Skill Combinations

Four-Player Offense

1. Divide players into groups of four. In each group, players act as center, quarterback or kicker, and two receivers.
2. A leader calls out combinations of movement and the players practice the play. Players may rotate positions or continue to practice one position.
3. Suggested play combinations follow:
   a. (Figure 4.24) Hike (center); punt (kicker); receive and carry (one receiver); block (other receiver); flag pull by center and kicker.
   b. (Figure 4.25) Hike (center); punt (kicker); receive and carry (one receiver); receive handoff or pitchout and carry (other receiver); flag pull by center and kicker.

Variation

Substitute a pass for each punt.

FIGURE 4.24	**FIGURE 4.25**
One Pattern for the Four-Player Offense.	A Second Pattern for the Four-Player Offense.

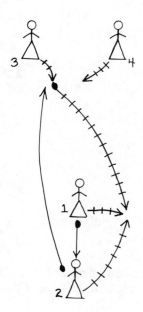

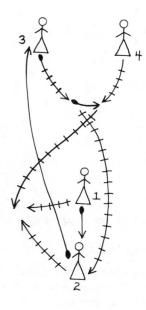

FIGURE   4.26
Six-Player Offense.

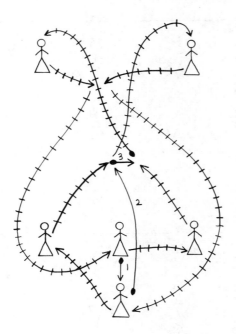

Six-Player Offense (Figure 4.26)

1. Divide players into groups of six. Each group includes a center, a quarterback, two ends, and two defenders who face the other players.
2. The center hikes the ball to the quarterback as the ends run down and across.
3. The quarterback passes the ball to either end as they cross over.
4. The player catching the ball either hands off or pitches out to the other end.
5. The player who receives the ball continues to a previously established goal line.
6. The two defending players try to pull the flag of the person with the ball.
7. Players rotate so quarterback and center become ends, ends become defenders, and defenders become center and quarterback.

LEAD-UP GAMES

Prisoner Ball (Grades 4–12)

This game allows players to practice punting and catching skills. All players should take a turn punting the ball.

Equipment

Football, cones, large playing space

FIGURE   4.27
Prisoner Ball.

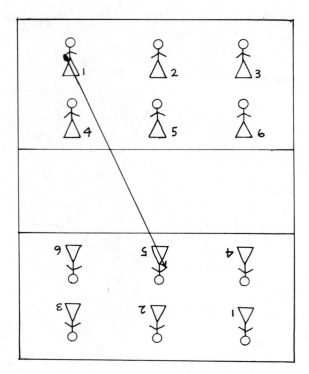

Procedures (Figure 4.27)

1. Players divide into two teams of six each. Each team takes one side of the field with a ten-yard neutral zone separating the teams. Assign each player a number (as shown in figure 4.27).

2. The player in the right back corner of one team begins the game with a punt. Each player on the back line punts, and then the catching team becomes the kicking team.

3. Before kicking the ball the punter calls out the number of an opponent.

4. Any player on the opposing team may catch the ball. If the other team fails to catch the ball and it lands in their area of the playing field, the player whose number was called crosses the neutral zone into the punting team's "prison" (behind the back line of the kicking team's playing area). A ball landing on a line or in the neutral zone must be kicked again.

5. When a team has caught two punts in a row, the player who has been in prison the longest returns and joins the team.

6. Play continues for a designated period of time, and the team with the fewest number of players in prison is declared the winner.

7. Player lines are rotated back to front when teams change from kicking to catching.

Base Football (Grades 4–12)

This game merges the skills of football and softball.

Equipment

Football, three bases, home plate

FIGURE   4.28
Base Football.

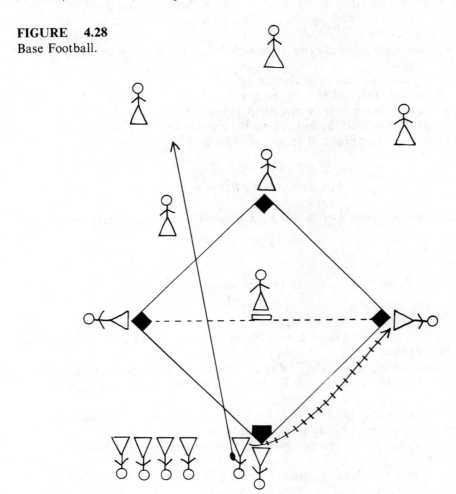

Procedures (Figure 4.28)

1. Position the players of the fielding team as in softball, with all players except the catcher behind an imaginary restraining line extending from first to third base.

2. Players on the offensive team line up behind the backstop. The first kicker or passer stands at home plate.
3. Play begins when the catcher gives the ball to the kicker/passer. This player may either punt or pass the ball into the field, anywhere beyond the restraining line.
4. Once the ball is put into play, the game is played as softball.
5. The fielding team either punts or passes the ball back to the catcher. When the ball reaches the catcher's hands, all offensive runners must return to, or remain on, the nearest base.
6. Base runners are out if they leave the base before the ball is released by the kicker/passer.
7. Kickers/passers are out when they
   a. kick or pass two foul balls in one at bat.
   b. step across home plate before releasing the ball.
   c. fail to pass or punt the ball beyond the restraining line.
8. Outs and runs are calculated according to softball rules.

Frisbee Football (Grades 4–12)

This game combines skills used in Frisbee and football and involves large numbers of players.

Equipment
Frisbee, colored vests, cones or other field markers

Procedures
1. Divide players into two equal teams. Players take positions scattered throughout the playing area.
2. Play begins with a toss of the Frisbee into the center of the playing area. The object of the game is to pass the Frisbee down field and across the goal line to score.
3. Any person catching the Frisbee must throw it before taking three steps (any player holding the Frisbee is allowed to take two steps).
4. If the opposing team intercepts the Frisbee, play moves in the opposite direction.
5. When a Frisbee lands on the ground, any player may pick it up and throw it.
6. If the Frisbee flies out of bounds or unsafe play occurs on one team, the other team gains possession of the Frisbee.
7. Each goal is worth one point. After one team scores a goal, the Frisbee is awarded to the opposite team to begin play in the middle of the field.

Keep-Away Football (Grades 4–12)

This game refines the students' passing and catching skills while helping players learn the game.

Equipment

Football

Procedures

1. Two teams of equal numbers line up on opposite sides of the field. One team begins the game with a hike from the center.
2. The team with the ball attempts to maneuver it into the opposite end zone.
3. The team with the ball may either pass or run until one of its ball carriers is tagged by an opponent. Once they tag a player, the opposing team gains possession of the ball.
4. If the ball hits the ground it is a free ball. Any player may pick it up, but the player who does so can only **pass** the ball to a teammate.
5. A player intercepting a pass may either run or pass the ball.
6. Touchdowns count as six points. After one team scores a touchdown, the other team is awarded the ball, on their half of the field, to begin play.

SKILL TESTS

Punt for Distance

Place three markers on the field at ten- to fifteen-yard intervals (space markers according to age and skill level of students). The participant stands several steps behind a restraining line and punts the ball into the field from behind the line. A foul occurs if the player steps across the line before punting the ball. Each player takes two trials. Score one point for a ball landing between the first and second markers; three points for a ball landing between the second and third markers; and five points for a ball landing beyond the third marker. The student's score is the total number of points earned in the two trials.

Pass for Distance

Place markers at five-yard intervals on the field, starting and ending at distances challenging the skill level of the students. The participant passes the ball from behind a restraining line. A foul occurs if the player steps across the line before passing the ball. Each player takes three trials. Score one point for each marker the ball passes. The score is the total number of points the participant earns in three trials.

Pass for Accuracy

Draw a circle with a diameter of five feet on a wall, with the lowest point one foot from the ground. Mark a throwing line twenty-five feet from the target for beginners and further away for more experienced players. The participant stands behind the throwing line and steps over the line with one foot, throwing the ball at the target. Allow five trials. Score one point for each throw that lands inside the target or on the target line.

Centering for Accuracy

Use the target described in the Pass for Accuracy skill test. Draw a line across the center of the target, dividing it into upper and lower halves. Mark a throwing line six to eight feet from the target. The participant stands facing away from the target and places the ball on the throwing line. With the ball on the ground, the player reaches out, grips the ball, and centers it back between the legs to hit the target. Allow five trials; score one point for each throw that lands within or on the lines of the lower half of the target. A foul occurs if the player picks up the ball before centering it.

Run for Speed (Figure 4.29)

Arrange markers in zigzag fashion ten, fifteen, twenty, twenty-five, and thirty yards from the starting line. On a signal, the participant, carrying the football, runs to the right of the first marker and weaves between the markers. After circling the fourth marker, the runner returns, overrunning the starting line. Score the time elapsed between the starting signal and the instant the player returns over the starting line. Record the time in seconds, to the nearest tenth.

Pass Receiving

The participant stands at a distance, determined by skill level, and attempts to catch five passes thrown by a teacher or able student. The score is the number of catchable passes caught. Repeat any passes that are extremely difficult or impossible to catch.

General Play

During a game, the teacher or an aide records statistics based on player action. Balls must be playable and catchable to count.

FIGURE   4.29
Run for Speed.

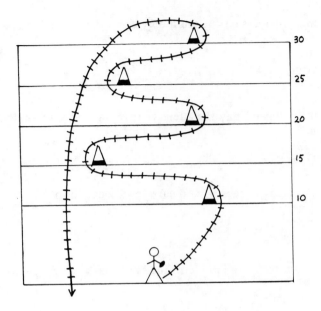

SITUATION   **TALLY**
Passes caught (receivers)
Passes dropped (receivers)
Passes thrown accurately (quarterback)
Passes thrown inaccurately (quarterback)
Flags pulled
Runs attempted
Yards gained
Accurate hikes
Correct offensive position
Correct defensive position

WRITTEN TEST

MULTIPLE CHOICE

1. What is the distance from one marker to the first-down marker on the football
   field?
   a. ten yards
   b. twenty yards
   c. five yards
   d. fifteen yards

2. How many players on one team may be on the field in an official flag football game?
   a. nine
   b. eleven
   c. seven
   d. six
3. How many downs may the offensive team take to earn another first down?
   a. four
   b. three
   c. one
   d. five
4. How many points does a team earn for a touchdown?
   a. seven
   b. two
   c. one
   d. six
5. If the defensive team intercepts the ball, which of the following would be wise strategy?
   a. try to score
   b. call a timeout
   c. block for the ball carrier
   d. both a and c
6. What should be called when a player illegally advances beyond the line of scrimmage before the ball is snapped?
   a. offside
   b. fumble
   c. illegal forward pass
   d. personal foul
7. What is the area between the goal line and end line called?
   a. the line of scrimmage
   b. the goal
   c. the end zone
   d. the safety zone
8. Which of the following defines the word *fumble?*
   a. centering the ball
   b. a ball not in play
   c. a dropped ball
   d. throwing a pass away
9. Which of the following is a defensive position?
   a. linebacker
   b. fullback
   c. half-back
   d. quarterback

10. A screen is executed by which of the following players?
    a. punter
    b. defense
    c. offense
    d. referee
11. A *safety* is best described by which of the following statements?
    a. An offensive player, with the ball, is tackled in the offense's own end zone.
    b. The ball is kicked out of the end zone.
    c. A defensive player recovers a fumble in the defense's own end zone.
    d. One player protects another player from danger.
12. What action is taken if any part of the ball carrier's body, other than feet or hands, touches the ground?
    a. The offense receives a five-yard penalty.
    b. The offense receives a fifteen-yard penalty.
    c. The ball is awarded to the other team.
    d. The ball is dead and the play ends.

COMPLETION

13. Diagram five basic pass patterns and name each.
14. List the yards assessed for each of the following penalties:
    a. Offside _____
    b. Unsportsmanlike conduct _____
    c. Abusive language _____
    d. Unnecessary roughness _____
    e. Illegal forward pass _____
    f. Securing flag to uniform _____
    g. Diving (feet leaving ground) to pull flag _____
15. Diagram or describe a zone defense employed by four players.

TEST KEY

1. b	10. c
2. a	11. a
3. a	12. d
4. d	13. Refer to figure 4.9.
5. d	14. a. five
6. a	b. fifteen
7. c	c. fifteen
8. c	d. fifteen
9. a	e. five
	f. fifteen
	g. fifteen

CHAPTER FIVE

SOCCER

Soccer is played worldwide by all ages, both males and females, and is suitable for coeducational play. This vigorous and challenging game can be easily modified to fit various sizes of indoor and outdoor spaces.

EQUIPMENT

Goalposts and nets
Balls

Vests
Field markers

SUGGESTIONS FOR INSTRUCTIONAL PROFICIENCY

1. Use a safe area for practice. To prevent injuries, enforce safety rules promptly and strictly, including penalizing rough behavior by players.
2. Teach students to take responsibility for where and how they kick the ball. (Kicking up or directly at another person is *dangerous*.)
3. Face the class away from direct sun for demonstration or drill practice.
4. Provide one ball for every two students when possible. Substitute balls of equal size when regulation balls are not available.
5. Teach regulation game rules and modify them when necessary for young or inexperienced players.
6. Use drills and practice strategies that build endurance so students can run continuously when playing regulation games.

TEACHING THE BASICS

The following progression is suggested:

1. **Dribbling:** Expect skill proficiency. Dribbling is the skill most basic to the game of soccer.

   Inside of foot
   Toe
   Outside of foot
   Combination of inside, toe, and outside of foot

2. **Passing and Trapping:** Like catching and throwing in other sports, passing and trapping should be taught together.

Passing	Trapping
Inside of foot	Sole-of-the-foot trap
Instep	Foot trap
Outside of foot	Body trap
Heading	Shin Trap

3. **Kicking**

    Punt
    Instep—executed for precision and redirection
    Instep—executed for power and accuracy
    Kickoff (place kick)
    Shooting
    Heel
    Corner

4. **Kicking and Trapping**
5. **Game Situations**

    Rules
    Tackling

6. **Strategy**

    Offensive strategy
    Defensive strategy

DRILLS

Dribble

Shuttle Dribble (Figure 5.1)

1. Form two file lines fifteen feet apart, with players facing each other.
2. The first player dribbles to the opposite line, passes the ball to the leader, and goes to the end of that line.
3. The player with the ball dribbles back to the opposite line. Players repeat the process until all return to their original places.

FIGURE   5.1
Shuttle Dribble.

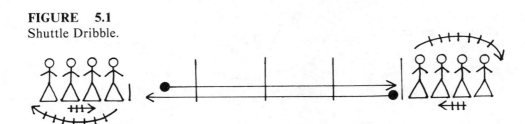

FIGURE   5.2
Straight-Line Dribble.

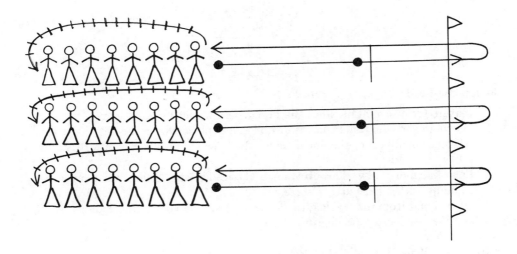

Straight-Line Dribble (Figure 5.2)

1. Assign four to five players to each of several file lines.
2. The first player in a file line dribbles the ball to a designated spot, turns around, dribbles back, passes the ball to the next player in line, and goes to the end of the line.
3. Each player in the line repeats this procedure until all players have dribbled a specified number of times.

Variation

Give each player a ball. The second person in line begins dribbling when the first player has moved two-thirds of the way to the end marker. Returning players move in a line five feet to the right so that players do not collide as they pass.

FIGURE   5.3
Follow-the-Leader.

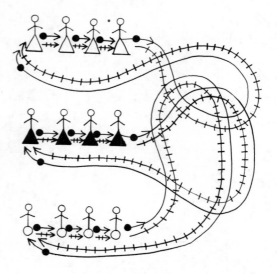

Follow-the-Leader (Snake) (Figure 5.3)

1. Players form several file lines and designate a leader for each line.
2. On command, the leader begins dribbling any place within the practice area.
3. All other members of the line dribble a ball, keeping it under control, as they follow the leader.
4. Each line moves in various directions. The leaders must maneuver to avoid colliding with other lines.
5. On a signal from the teacher, the leader in each file goes to the end of the line and the next person becomes the leader.

Direction Dribble (Figure 5.4)

1. Players form several file lines.
2. The first player in a file line dribbles to a marker, makes a wide sweep, and dribbles to the end of the line.
3. When the dribbler passes the marker, the next player begins.
4. Dribblers move continuously until all participants have completed the pattern a designated number of times. Dribblers must be alert to avoid collisions.

FIGURE   5.4
Direction Dribble.

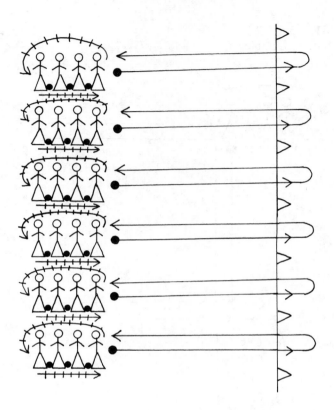

FIGURE   5.5
Maneuver Dribble.

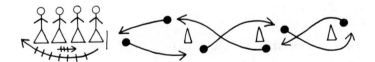

Maneuver Dribble (Figure 5.5)

1. Players form several file lines.
2. The first player in each file line dribbles around several markers and then returns to the starting position.
3. The next player repeats the process as the returning player goes to the end of the line.
4. Each player in line takes a turn to dribble.

FIGURE 5.6
Four-Square Dribble.

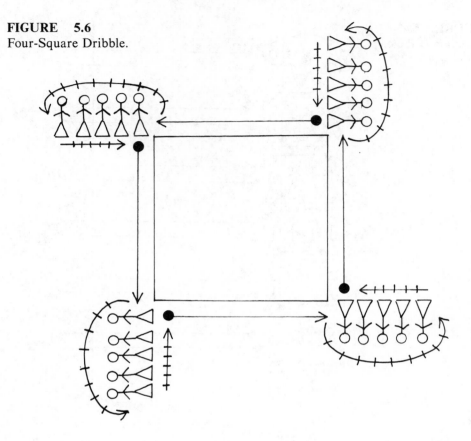

Four-Square Dribble (Figure 5.6)

1. Select a square playing area large enough to allow four dribblers room to maneuver.
2. Form four file lines, one at each corner of the square practice area.
3. The first player in each line dribbles counterclockwise along the border of the square to the next line.
4. The first player passes the ball to the next person in the line. The original dribbler then moves to the end of this line.
5. Dribbling continues until all players have returned to their original line.

FIGURE   5.7
Box Dribble.

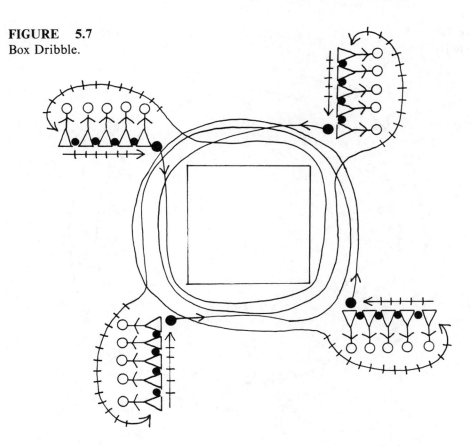

Box Dribble (Figure 5.7)

1. Players form four file lines, one at each corner of a large, square practice area. Each player has a ball.
2. The first person in each line dribbles counterclockwise along the borders of the square.
3. When dribblers return to starting positions, they move to the end of the line and the next players repeat the procedure.
4. Dribbling continues until all players return to their original positions.

FIGURE   5.8
Circle Dribble.

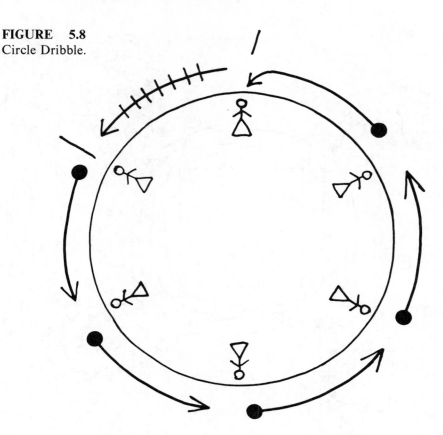

Circle Dribble (Figure 5.8)

1. Five or more players station themselves around a circle, facing outward.
2. One player dribbles the ball completely around the outside of the circle and stops to pass the ball to the next player on the right.
3. The player with the ball repeats the process and the dribbler returns to the circle.
4. Practice continues until each person has dribbled around the circle two or more times.

Variation (Figure 5.9)

The person dribbling the ball maneuvers in and out around each person in the circle. If enough players form the circle, two or three players could begin dribbling from equal distances around the circle.

FIGURE 5.9
Variation on the
Circle Dribble.

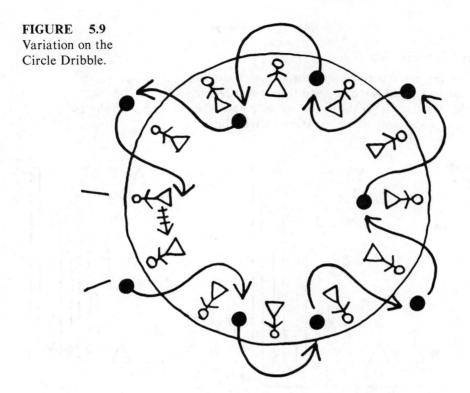

The 5–20 Dribble (Figure 5.10)

1. Lay out a practice area with a starting line. Mark the starting line with a starting point and four markers placed at five-yard intervals.
2. Each player stands with a ball behind the starting line.
3. The first person dribbles up even with the five-yard marker and back to the starting line. Without interrupting movement, the dribbler moves over five yards and dribbles up even with the ten-yard marker and back to the starting line.
4. The process is repeated as the dribbler moves to each succeeding marker and back to the end of the line.
5. Another dribbler begins each time the preceding player has reached the second marker.
6. Practice stops when each player has repeated the drill twice.

Passing and Trapping

Partner Pass and Trap (Figure 5.11)

1. Two players, standing at least five yards apart, face each other.
2. One player passes the ball and the other player traps it.
3. The trapping player then becomes the passer. Players alternate roles as they practice various passing and trapping techniques.

FIGURE 5.10
The 5–20 Dribble.

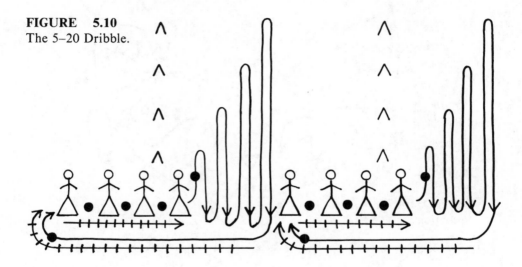

FIGURE 5.11
Partner Pass and Trap.

FIGURE   5.12
Triad Pass and Trap.

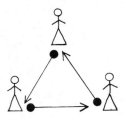

FIGURE   5.13
Leader Pass and Trap.

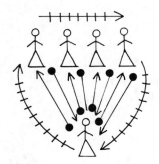

Triad Pass and Trap (Figure 5.12)

1. Three players form a triangle.
2. Each player passes the ball counterclockwise to the next player, who then traps the ball.
3. As players acquire skill, they move back to expand the size of the triangle. Players may practice a variety of passing and trapping techniques in this formation.

Leader Pass and Trap (Figure 5.13)

1. A leader faces several players in a line five yards away.
2. The leader passes the ball to the first player in line, who traps the ball and passes it back to the leader.
3. The leader repeats the same procedure with each player along the line.
4. When the last player passes the ball back to the leader, players rotate counterclockwise and a new leader moves into place.
5. Players repeat the drill until all players have acted as leader.

Shuttle Pass and Trap (Figure 5.14)

1. Players form file lines facing each other.
2. The first person passes the ball straight to the first player in the opposite line.
3. The receiving player traps the ball.
4. The receiving player then passes the ball straight back to the first person in the opposite line and goes to the end of the same line.
5. The receiving passer traps the ball, passes it again, and moves to the end of the same line. Players repeat the process until all are in their original places.

FIGURE   5.14
Shuttle Pass and Trap.

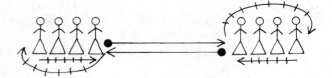

FIGURE   5.15
Circle Pass and Trap.

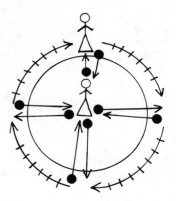

Circle Pass and Trap (Figure 5.15)

1. Partners face each other approximately ten yards apart. One person stands on the outside of a circle and the other stands in the middle.
2. The player in the middle of the circle passes to the outside, where the partner traps the ball and passes it back.
3. The center partner traps the ball and passes it back out, but farther around the circle. The outside partner moves to trap the ball.
4. Players repeat the process until the outside partner is back to starting position.
5. Partners exchange places and the drill begins again.

Moving Pass and Trap (Figure 5.16)

1. Players form three file lines five to ten yards apart. Each player in the left line has a ball.
2. The first player in each line moves forward to form a team of three. This team moves the ball downfield to a designated place.
3. The player from the left line passes ahead to the player from the middle line.
4. The middle player traps the ball and passes it ahead to the player from the right line.

FIGURE   5.16
Moving Pass and Trap.

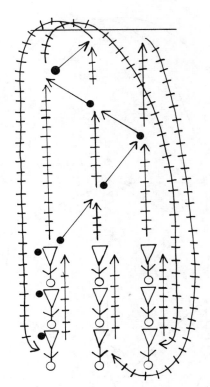

5. The right player traps the ball and passes it ahead to the middle player.
6. The middle player traps the ball and passes it ahead to the left player.
7. The left player traps the ball, and the team repeats the process until the players have reached the designated stopping line.
8. Three new players begin after the preceding group passes the ball three times.
9. After reaching the end line, players return to the starting lines, rotating one line to the left. (Be sure these players move to the outside of the playing field to avoid interfering with moving players.)

Dribble, Pass, and Trap (Figure 5.17)

1. Approximately ten players line up side by side.
2. The middle player (number 1 in figure 5.17) acts as passer, and takes position with several balls approximately five yards downfield. Another middle player (number 2) acts as trapper-passer and remains on the starting line.

FIGURE   5.17

Dribble, Pass, and Trap.

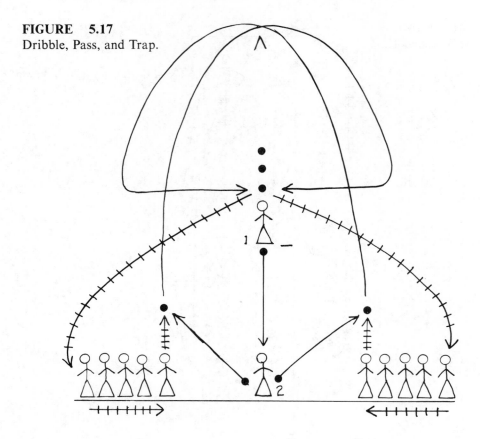

3. The players on either side of player number 2 move ten yards away from the middle, creating two lines.
4. Middle player 1 passes a ball downfield to player 2, who traps the ball and passes it to one of the lines on either side. The first player in that line receives the pass, dribbles downfield twenty to thirty yards, moves around a cone in the center of the field, and returns to the position directly behind player 1. The dribbler leaves the ball behind player 1 and runs to the end of the opposite line.
5. Player 1 passes another ball to player 2, who traps it and passes it to the first player in the opposite line.
6. This alternating procedure continues until each player has had a turn dribbling the ball. The first two players in each line then take the places of players 1 and 2, and players 1 and 2 move to the end of each receiving line.
7. Players repeat the drill with new players in the middle positions.
8. Play continues until all players have had a turn in positions 1 and 2.

FIGURE   5.18
Heading Partner Pass.

FIGURE   5.19
Partner Kick for Distance.

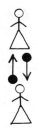

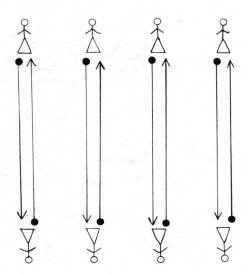

Heading Partner Pass (Figure 5.18)

1. Partners face each other.
2. One partner tosses the ball to the other, who heads the ball back. (Light balls might be used at first.)
3. Partners continuously head the ball back and forth.

Heading Triangle Pass

1. Three players form a triangle.
2. The first player tosses the ball clockwise to the next player. The three players continue to head the ball clockwise to each other.

Variation

Four players form a square and follow the same procedure.

Kicking

Partner Kick for Distance (Figure 5.19)

1. Establish a line of direction. Rows of partners face each other, leaving enough space to allow safe kicking.
2. One partner in each pair kicks the ball as far as possible.
3. The other partner retrieves the ball and kicks it back.

FIGURE   5.20
Kick for Accuracy.

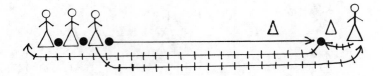

FIGURE   5.21
Triad Kick for Accuracy.

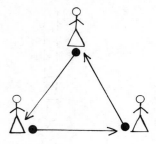

Kick for Accuracy (Figure 5.20)

1. Players kick at a target, such as a cone.
2. Kickers practice various kicks at several distances.
3. A nonkicking partner retrieves the ball and returns it to the kicking line.
4. After five attempts, the kicker becomes a retriever and a new kicker repeats the drill.

Triad Kick for Accuracy (Figure 5.21)

1. Three players position themselves in a triangle approximately ten feet apart from one another.
2. Players kick the ball counterclockwise from player to player.
3. Kickers practice various kicks at several distances.

Shooting (Figure 5.22)

1. Players form a file line facing a goal area thirty to fifty yards away.
2. Each player in turn dribbles toward the goal area and shoots. The same player retrieves the ball and dribbles to the end of the line to repeat the drill.

FIGURE   5.22
Shooting.

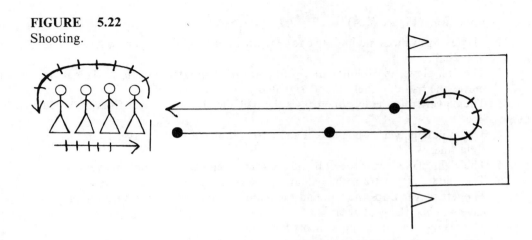

FIGURE   5.23
Shooting and Goalie Return.

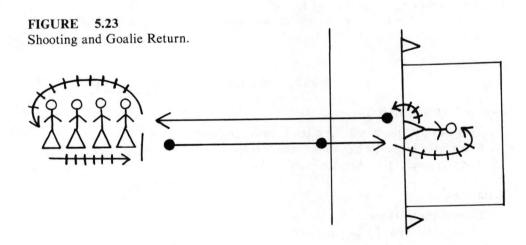

Shooting and Goalie Return (Figure 5.23)

1. Players form a file line facing a goal area thirty to fifty yards from the goal line. A goalkeeper stands ready to defend the goal and return the ball.
2. The first player dribbles toward the goal and shoots.
3. The goalie attempts to stop the shot, then retrieves the ball and dribbles back to the line to pass the ball to the next player.
4. The player who shot for the goal replaces the goalkeeper.
5. The next player in line dribbles downfield to shoot as the former goalie moves to the end of the line.

Shoot and Run (Figure 5.24)

1. Players form three file lines five to ten yards apart. Each player in the left line has a ball.
2. The first player in each line moves forward to form a team of three. This team moves the ball downfield to a designated place.
3. The player from the left line passes the ball ahead to the player from the middle line.
4. The middle player traps the ball and passes it ahead to the player from the right line.
5. The right player traps the ball and passes it ahead to the middle player.
6. The middle player traps the ball and passes it ahead to the left player.
7. The left player traps the ball and the team repeats the process until the players have reached the goal area.
8. The player nearest the goal shoots for a goal.
9. One player retrieves the ball and all three players move to avoid the next threesome.
10. After returning to the starting line, players move one line to the left.
11. Additional teams of three repeat the drill until all players have dribbled downfield.

Kicking and Trapping

Partner Kick and Trap (Figure 5.25)

1. Two players, standing at least ten yards apart, face each other.
2. One player kicks the ball to the other player, who traps it.
3. The trapping player then becomes the kicker.

Variations

1. Change the distance the ball is kicked.
2. Change the type of kick employed.

Leader Kick and Trap (Figure 5.26)

1. A leader stands at least ten yards in front of a line of several players.
2. The leader passes the ball to the first player in the line, who traps the ball and kicks it back.
3. The same procedure is repeated with each player along the line.
4. When the last player in line kicks the ball back to the leader, players rotate counterclockwise and a new leader emerges.
5. Players repeat the drill until all players have acted as leader.

FIGURE   5.24
Shoot and Run.

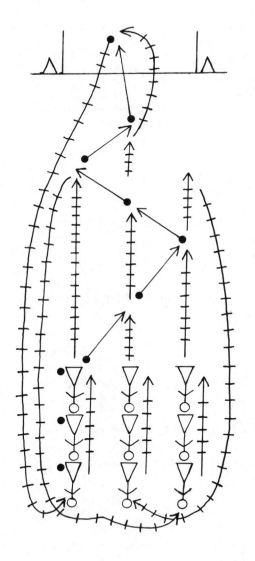

FIGURE   5.25
Partner Kick and Trap.

FIGURE   5.26
Leader Kick and Trap.

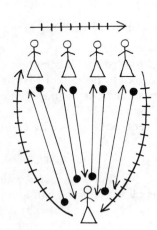

FIGURE   5.27
Four-Square Kick and Trap.

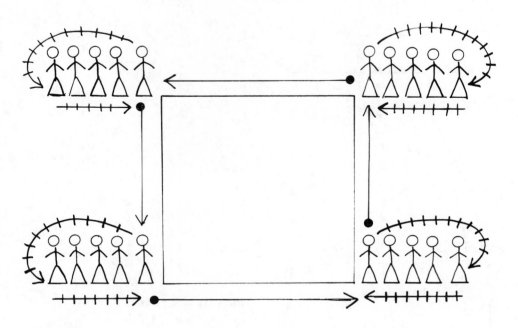

Four-Square Kick and Trap (Figure 5.27)

1. Players form four file lines, one at each corner of a square practice area.
2. The first person in each line kicks the ball counterclockwise to the next file line and goes to the end of that line.
3. The second person in each file line traps the ball and kicks it counterclockwise to the next file line.
4. Players continue kicking and trapping until all return to their original positions.

Wall Kick and Trap (Figure 5.28)

1. Four to six players face a wall.
2. One player puts the ball into play with a kick to the wall.
3. Any other player traps the rebounding ball, then kicks the ball back to the wall.
4. Play continues in this manner until a designated time period elapses.

Game Situations

Tackling Shuttle (Figure 5.29)

1. Players form two file lines facing each other. One line will dribble the ball, the other line will tackle.
2. The first person in the dribbling line dribbles straight ahead, trying to get around the tackler coming from the opposite line.
3. The tackler tries to gain possession of the ball, while the dribbler tries to keep it. Whichever player—tackler or dribbler—ends up with the ball then passes it back to the next person in the dribbling line. (The ball always starts from the dribbling line.)
4. Each player goes to the end of the opposite line.
5. Players repeat the process until all players return to their original places.

FIGURE   5.28
Wall Kick and Trap.

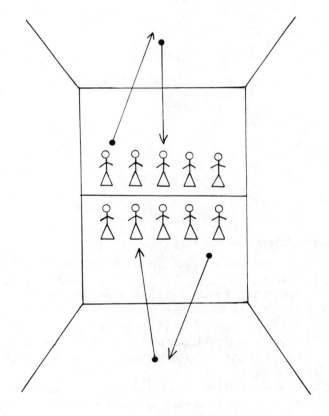

FIGURE   5.29
Tackling Shuttle.

FIGURE   5.30
Tackling-Moving Pass and Trap.

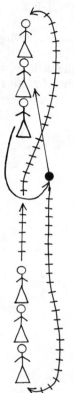

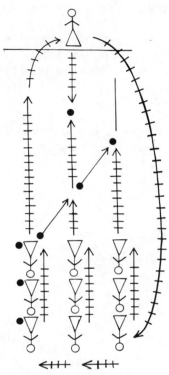

Tackling-Moving Pass and Trap (Figure 5.30)

1. Players form three file lines five to ten yards apart. Each player in the left line has a ball.
2. The first person in each of the lines moves forward to form a team of three. This team moves the ball downfield to a designated place. A fourth player takes a defensive position in front of the moving lines.
3. The player from the left line passes ahead to the player in the middle line.
4. The middle player traps the ball and passes it ahead to the player from the right line.
5. The right player traps the ball and passes it ahead to the middle player.
6. The middle player traps the ball and passes it ahead to the left player.
7. The left player traps the ball and the threesome repeats the process until the players reach the end line.

FIGURE   5.31
Tackling Dribble,
Pass and Trap.

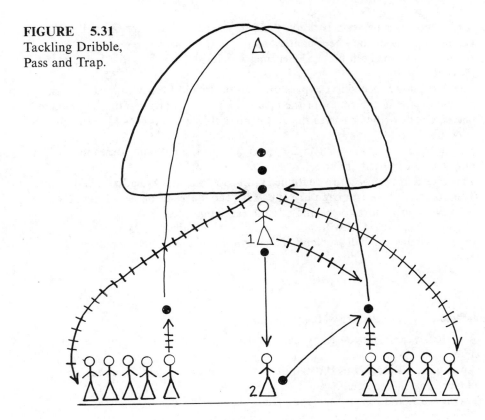

8. The defensive player tackles until gaining possession of the ball or until the offensive players reach the end line.
9. Three new players begin after the preceding group passes the ball three times.
10. The player from the left side of the moving line becomes the defensive player for the next group.
11. The other two players move out of the way of oncoming players and return to the starting line, rotating one line to the left. The defensive player moves into the starting line on the right.
12. The drill continues until all players have acted as the defensive player.

Tackling Dribble, Pass and Trap (Figure 5.31)

1. Approximately ten players line up side by side.
2. The middle player (number 1 in figure 5.31) acts as passer, taking several balls approximately five yards downfield. Another middle player (number 2) acts as trapper-passer.
3. The players on either side of player number 2 move ten yards away from the middle, creating two lines.

4. Middle player 1 passes a ball downfield to player 2, who traps the ball and passes it to one of the lines on either side.
5. After passing the ball, player 1 becomes a defensive player and attempts to tackle.
6. The first player receiving the pass dribbles downfield twenty to thirty yards, around a cone in the center of the field, and back to a position directly behind player 1. The dribbler leaves the ball behind player 1 and runs to the end of the opposite line.
7. Player 1 passes again to player 2. Player 2 traps the ball and passes to the first player in the opposite line.
8. This alternating procedure continues until each player has had a turn dribbling. The first two players in each line then take the places of players 1 and 2, and players 1 and 2 move to the end of each receiving line.
9. Players repeat the drill with new players in the middle positions.
10. Play continues until all participants have acted as the defensive player.

Strategy

Open-Field Offensive Strategy (Figure 5.32)

1. An offensive unit moves down the field, passing the ball to the outside of the field.
2. An outside player passes the ball into the center of the field. The receiving player shoots at the goal.
3. Players turn and repeat the action from the opposite side of the field.
4. Play continues with players exchanging positions or varying the origin of the play.

Offensive Maneuvering Strategy

1. An offensive unit moves down the field, passing around cones or other markers.
2. The unit maneuvers the ball to the center of the field. A player in the center shoots at the goal.

Planned-Play Offensive Strategy

1. Offensive players practice specific plays designed to produce a score.
2. Practice continues until proficiency is achieved.

Defensive Strategy

1. Add defensive players to the offensive drill shown in figure 5.32 and in the Planned-Play Offensive.
2. Practice until defensive players perfect their skills.

FIGURE   5.32
Open-Field Offensive Strategy.

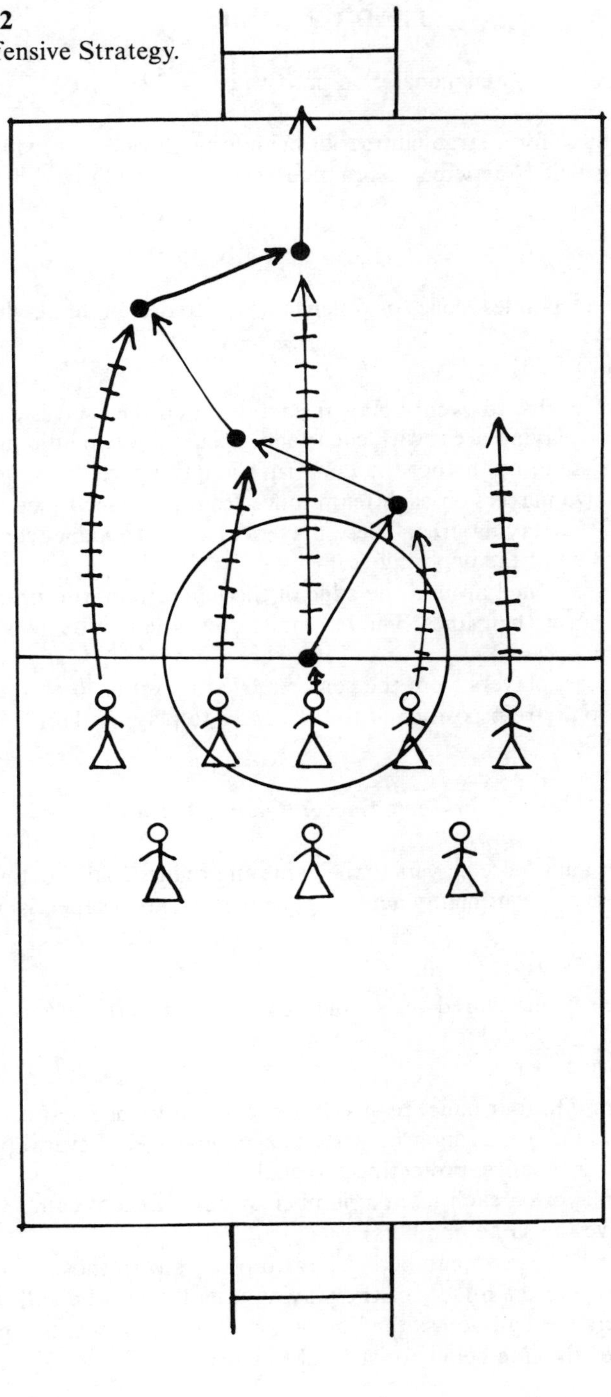

LEAD-UP GAMES

Diagonal Soccer (Grades 4–12)

This game is suitable for a large number of beginning players in a gymnasium or outside on a playing field. Participants practice basic ball-handling skills in a confined area.

Equipment

Soccer ball, vests or pinnies, cones or other markers to designate playing area

Procedures (Figure 5.33)

1. Two teams of twelve to twenty players each position themselves around a square or rectangular playing area, with each team occupying two adjoining boundary lines. Players stand no further than an arm's length apart.
2. On a signal, two players on each team move from position *A* (see figure 5.33) to the center of the playing area. These players attempt to maneuver the ball across either line of the opposing team.
3. The players positioned around the edge of the field attempt to prevent the ball from crossing over their lines. The ball must cross the line below waist-level to score.
4. After each score, players from the center move to position *B* on their team, and new players come from position *A* to the center to play the ball.

Four-Team Soccer (Grades 4–12)

Four-Team Soccer adds more players to the game and refines goal-shooting skills. Large numbers of players are continually active under the teacher's supervision.

Equipment

Soccer ball, three sets of colored vests, cones or other markers for goal

Procedures (Figure 5.34)

1. Divide players into four equal teams. Each team positions itself on a different side of a rectangular playing area with its own goal area. Several players on each team act as goalies, protecting the goal.
2. Assign each player on each team a number by asking each team to count off (all teams have the same numbers).
3. The teacher calls out two numbers. The two players with those numbers from each team move to the middle of the playing area to play the ball. Any team that maneuvers the ball across the line of any other team scores a point. (The ball must cross the line below waist-level to score.)

FIGURE   5.33
Diagonal Soccer.

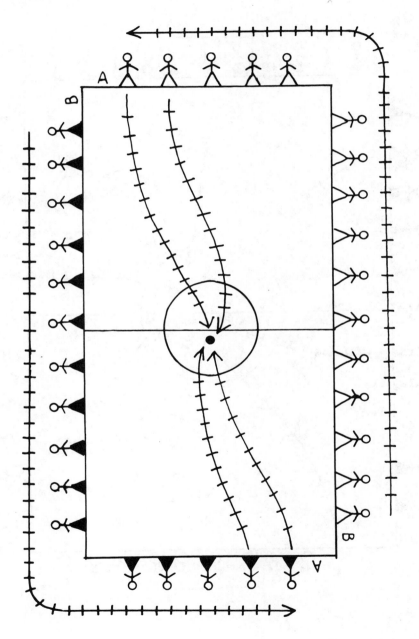

FIGURE   5.34
Four-Team Soccer.

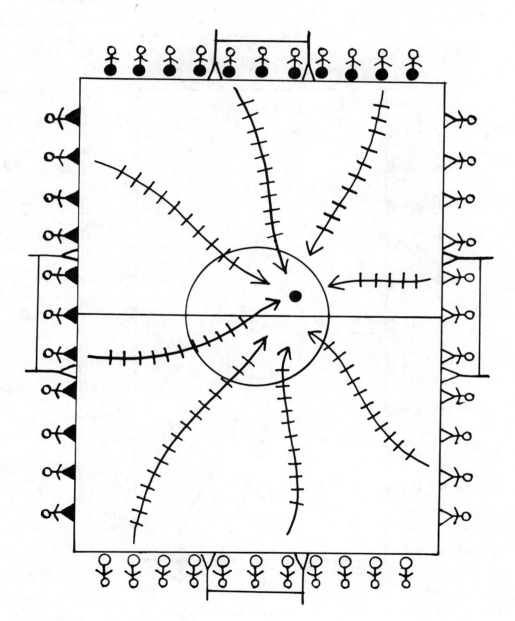

4. Players return to their places and the teacher calls two more numbers.
5. Players may not use their hands. Teachers should enforce all safety precautions.
6. Play continues in this manner until one team earns a designated number of points or until a certain amount of time elapses.

Variation

One goalie is assigned to defend the goal on each line. Rotate players frequently to goalie position.

Number Soccer (Grades 4–12)

Number Soccer helps students practice keeping the ball in bounds.

Equipment

Soccer ball, vests or pinnies

Procedures (Figure 5.35)
1. Divide the class into two teams. Line the teams up on opposite sides of the field or gymnasium, facing each other.
2. Players on each team count off so each player has a number.
3. The teacher places a ball in the middle of the playing area.
4. The teacher calls either one or two numbers, and the players on each team with those numbers move to the middle of the field to play the ball.
5. The players on the field try to move the ball across the line of the opposing team, keeping it below waist-level. Players positioned along the sidelines try to prevent a score.
6. Players may not use their hands.
7. At the end of one minute, or when one team has scored, the teacher blows a whistle and players on the field return to their respective lines.
8. The teacher calls new numbers and those players enter the playing area to begin play.

Corner Soccer (Grades 4–12)

This game allows participants to maneuver the ball and avoid defensive players.

Equipment

Soccer ball, vests or pinnies, cones or markers

FIGURE 5.35
Number Soccer.

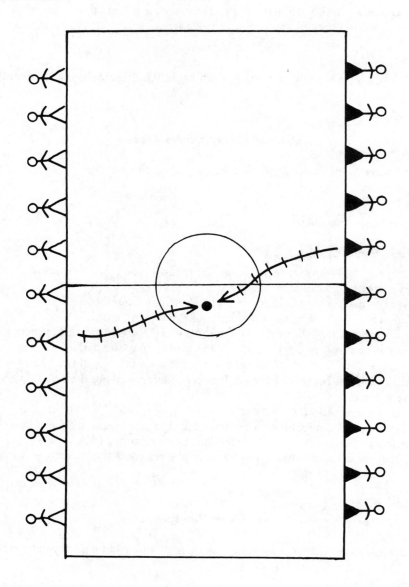

Procedures (Figure 5.36)

1. Two teams position themselves along opposite sides of the playing field or gymnasium. On each team, the players divide equally and move to either side of position *B* (see figure 5.36).
2. On a signal, the two players on each team stationed at the *A* positions (at the corners of the field) move to the center of the playing area.
3. The teacher rolls the ball in any direction and the players in the center attempt to score by maneuvering the ball across the line of the opposing team.
4. The ball must cross the line below waist-level and players may not use their hands.
5. After each score, or after several minutes of playing time, all players on the line move one position away from *B* towards *A*. The players in the center move back into their lines at position *B*.
6. Four new corner players move from the *A* positions to the center and play resumes.

Goalie Soccer (Grades 4–12)

This game allows more experienced players to practice scoring and capturing the ball.

Equipment

Two soccer balls, vests or pinnies, cones or other markers

Procedures (Figure 5.37)

1. Divide players into four equal teams. Two teams are designated as offense and two as defense. One offensive and one defensive team are positioned on each half of a regulation soccer field.
2. A separate game is played on each half of the field.
3. Each offensive team is positioned around their half of the center circle.
4. Each defensive team is scattered throughout the remaining playing area on their half of the field.
5. Each offensive team appoints a goalie to stand inside their half of the center circle. Each defensive team chooses a goalie to play in the regulation goal area.
6. The offensive goalie puts the ball into play. The offensive team then tries to score a regulation goal. The defensive team tries to capture the ball and shoot it inside the center circle.
7. If players from the offensive team score a goal, or if the defensive team can maneuver the ball into the half-circle area defended by the offensive goalie, the two teams change positions. However, only offensive teams earn a point when they score a goal. The defensive team simply earns the chance to play offense, and play begins again with a new offensive team.

FIGURE   5.36
Corner Soccer.

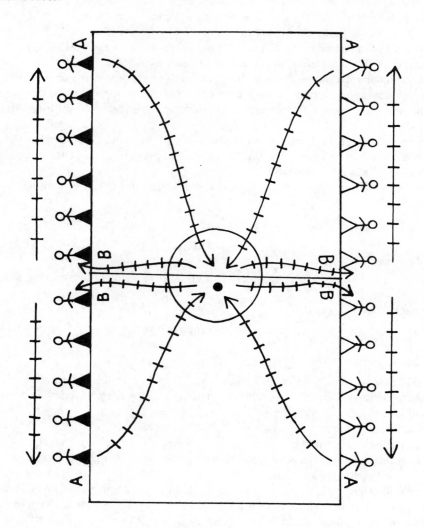

FIGURE   5.37
Goalie Soccer.

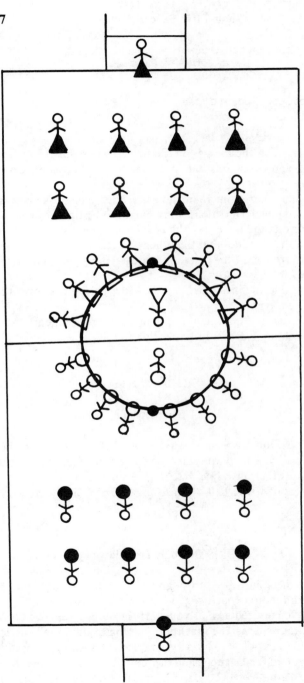

Whole Field Soccer (Grades 8–12)

This game allows the teacher to monitor students learning how to play soccer.

Equipment

Soccer ball, three sets of colored vests

Procedures (Figure 5.38)

1. Four teams position themselves on the field. Two teams take positions on the playing field, and two teams line up facing each other on opposite sides of the playing area.
2. Play stops when players make mistakes or when questions arise so that the teacher may make clarifications. Play may also be limited to specific skills.
3. The two teams on the field play the ball until the whistle blows. At this time, they move to the sidelines and the other two teams move on to the playing field. Time periods are left to the discretion of the teacher so that all teams get equal playing time.
4. The teams on the sidelines must not allow the ball to pass over their lines. If it does, they lose a point.
5. Any team that asks a specific question or makes a pertinent observation scores a point. This technique draws full attention to the game.

SKILL TESTS

Timed Dribble

Time the player's dribbling speed over a fifty-yard distance. Signal the player to start by lowering your raised arm as you start the stopwatch. Stop the watch when the player's first foot crosses the finish line. Record the time to the nearest tenth of a second. The player must contact the ball at least once in each five-yard section of the fifty-yard distance.

Obstacle Dribble

Time the player's dribbling speed through an obstacle course. Place five cones at six-yard intervals with the first cone five yards from the starting line. Signal the player to start by lowering your raised arm as you start the stopwatch. The player legally dribbles the ball to either side of the first cone, coming around the cone to dribble to the opposite side of the next cone. The player repeats this zigzag procedure through the course, turning around the last cone and dribbling back to the starting line in the same manner. Stop the watch when the player's first foot crosses the finish line. Repeat the test if a player fails to dribble around any cone or illegally plays the ball.

FIGURE   5.38
Whole Field Soccer.

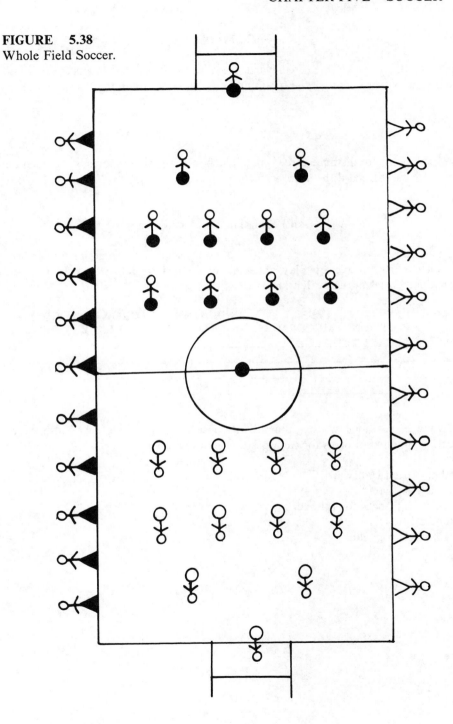

Goal Shoot

Each player starts from a line fifteen yards from the goal area and shoots the ball into the goal. The player's score is the total number of goals made in ten kicks.

Punt

Each player punts for distance three times. The best of the three scores is recorded for grading purposes. Record the score in feet.

Game Situation Checklist

Using a checklist, evaluate each player in a game situation. Record a plus for superior play, a checkmark for average play, and a minus for unsatisfactory play. Include the following categories in the evaluation:

NAME	PLAY AT POSITION	PASS ACCURACY	DRIBBLING CONTROL	THROW-IN ACCURACY	GOALIE DEFENSE

Identify player positions by using pinnies with positions marked on front and back, or by creating unique uniforms for each position. For example:

Basketball vests for forwards
T-shirts for halfbacks
Baseball stirrup socks for fullbacks
Flag football ties for centers
Baseball caps for goalies

WRITTEN TEST

MATCHING

a. save
b. corner kick
c. dribbling
d. field goal
e. halfbacks
f. goalie box

g. forwards
h. free kick
i. goalkeeper
j. goal kick
k. sideline
l. recovery

m. goal line
n. penalty area
o. kickoff
p. throw-in
q. punt
r. tackling

_____ 1. The boundary line at each end of the field
_____ 2. Moving the ball using short kicks
_____ 3. A defender's place kick taken after an offensive player has kicked the ball out of bounds over the goal line and outside the goalposts
_____ 4. Action that puts the ball back into play after it goes out of bounds over the touch lines
_____ 5. The territory in front of the goal where the goalkeeper may handle the ball
_____ 6. Place kick taken at the center of the field to begin the game
_____ 7. A direct free kick by the attacking player after a defender kicks the ball out of bounds over the goal line
_____ 8. Players whose main responsibility is to score
_____ 9. A goalkeeper's play that prevents a goal from being scored
_____ 10. The only player allowed to use hands
_____ 11. The score made when the ball crosses the goal line under the crossbar
_____ 12. A place kick by the opposing team after an infraction has been committed

MULTIPLE CHOICE

13. Which of the following best defines the term *marking?*
    a. passing the ball from the wing area to the center
    b. propelling the ball with the forehead
    c. guarding an opponent
    d. none of the above
14. Which of the following best describes how a throw-in is performed?
    a. with both feet on the ground and the ball at least waist-high
    b. with one hand and both feet on the ground
    c. with both hands overhead and both feet in contact with ground
    d. in any manner, as long as the player is behind touch line

15. Which players form the line of defense in front of the goalie?
    a. midfielders
    b. wings
    c. halfbacks
    d. fullbacks
16. Which of the following is a term that means to advance the ball with the foot using short ground kicks from one player to another?
    a. juggle
    b. pass
    c. punt
    d. kick in
17. Which team tries to score goals?
    a. offense
    b. defense
    c. both of the above
    d. neither of the above

TRUE OR FALSE

T   F   18. Eleven players and one goalie comprise a soccer team.
T   F   19. A penalty kick may be taken anywhere within five yards of the penalty spot.
T   F   20. **Tackling** is trying to take the ball away from an opponent.
T   F   21. A corner kick is taken by the attacking team.
T   F   22. **Juggling** is using the forehead to propel the ball.
T   F   23. **Obstruction** is a violation committed by an offensive player who is ahead of the ball without two defenders between the goal and the player.
T   F   24. On a throw-in, all players must be ten yards away.
T   F   25. The penalty for holding is a direct free kick.

TEST KEY

MATCHING

1. m	5. n	9. a
2. c	6. o	10. i
3. j	7. b	11. d
4. p	8. g	12. h

MULTIPLE CHOICE

13. c
14. c
15. d
16. b
17. a

TRUE OR FALSE

18. F
19. F
20. T
21. T
22. F
23. F
24. T
25. T

CHAPTER SIX

SOFTBALL

Fast-pitch softball is an active game when played by highly skilled players. Slow-pitch softball has evolved in response to the inability of most students to master pitching. The emphasis in this chapter is to create a more active game for all players.

EQUIPMENT

Softballs: regulation, indoor, and fleeceballs
Bases, pitcher's plate
Gloves
Bats
Chest protectors, face masks
Backstops, field markings

SUGGESTIONS FOR INSTRUCTIONAL PROFICIENCY

1. Provide one softball for every two people, if possible.
2. Provide indoor softballs when practicing inside.
3. Use a fleeceball, or another softer ball, to alleviate fear when introducing catching drills.
4. Use progressive warm-ups and drills to prevent soreness and injuries to legs and throwing arms.
5. Allow ample space between students, and organize the class so all students throw and bat in the same direction.
6. Practice skills with students facing away from the sun.
7. Position those waiting to bat behind the backstop or a protective fence. If neither is available, have batters wait on the first base side of the infield.
8. Do not allow students to throw the bat after batting.
9. Require the catcher to wear protective equipment.
10. Use only proven pitchers, or the teacher, in game situations to increase player activity.
11. Modify playing rules to maximize time on task.
12. Arrange to use multiple diamonds to avoid player collisions.
13. Instruct students to "call" for fly balls.
14. Require students to account for each piece of equipment at the end of class.

TEACHING THE BASICS

The following progression is suggested:

1. **Throwing and Catching**: Teach these skills together.
2. **Fielding**: Practice fielding balls that come from various directions at different speeds.

> Infield
> Outfield

3. **Pitching**: Teach all students the mechanics of pitching.

> Simple underhand
> Windmill
> Whip (half-windmill)

4. **Batting**

> Grip
> Full swing
> Bunt

5. **Strategy**: Verbally set up gamelike situations and ask players what they would do. Then create the situation and allow players to execute the play.

DRILLS

Throwing and Catching

Target Throw

1. Place targets of various sizes and heights on a wall (indoors or outdoors).
2. Students throw at the target from several challenging distances and directions.

Straight-Line Throw and Catch (Figure 6.1)

1. All players form two straight lines facing each other. The distance between players is determined by their skill.
2. Partners practice throwing and catching with each other.

FIGURE   6.1
Straight-Line Throw and Catch.

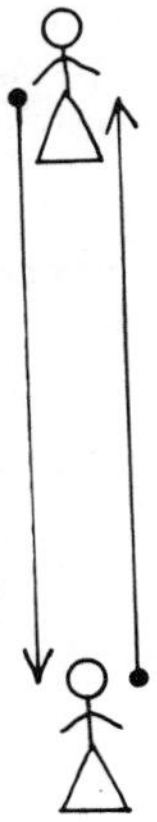

FIGURE   6.2
Zigzag Throw and Catch.

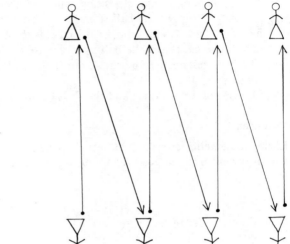

Zigzag Throw and Catch (Figure 6.2)

1. Players form two lines facing each other. The distance between players is determined by their skill.
2. One player on the end of either line throws the ball to the player directly across in the other line.
3. The receiving player throws the ball diagonally to the next player in the opposite line.
4. Players continue throwing in the same zigzag pattern.
5. The first player starts a second ball when the first ball reaches the middle of the line.

Base Practice Throw and Catch (Figure 6.3)

1. Assign one player to each base and to home plate.
2. The catcher throws a ground ball to any spot in the infield. The player nearest the ball fields it and throws it to first. The first baseman throws the ball to second, the second baseman to third, and the third baseman throws it home.
3. Players rotate one position toward the catcher after completing the throwing circuit.

Fielding

Infield Practice

1. Assign players to infield positions and one player to home plate.
2. A "batter" throws the ball from home plate, then attempts to run to each base in order. The nearest infield player fields the ball and throws it to first base. The infield players throw the ball to each base in turn.
3. The base runner may be called out if the ball reaches first base before the runner.
4. Players rotate positions and the drill begins again.

Variation

Either the teacher or a student bats the ball from home plate. Fielders catch the ball and throw in a designated sequence or as dictated in a situation called out by the batter.

FIGURE   6.3
Base Practice Throw and Catch.

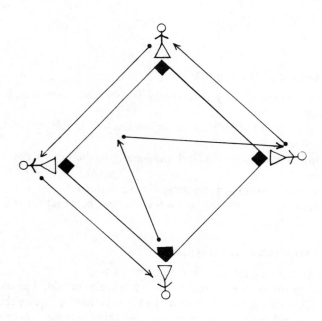

Outfield Practice

1. Students stand in an open area at least twenty feet away from one student. This student continually throws or hits fly balls.
2. Players catch the balls and throw them back to an assistant, who stands close by the hitter to feed the ball back.

Fungo Batting

1. Assign teams to fielding positions on several diamonds.
2. A teacher or leader hits the ball, simulating game situations and allowing players to practice skills.

Pitching

Straight Line

1. Players form two straight lines facing each other. Partners practice pitching and catching.
2. Students should practice at game distance. (This distance may be modified according to the ages and skills of students.)

Simulation

1. A pitcher and a catcher pitch and catch the ball.
2. Another student stands in the batting stance to give the pitcher a strike zone. Students rotate places after every five pitches.

Batting

Batting Tee

1. When skilled pitching is unavailable, use a batting tee for students learning to hit.
2. Students work in groups of three with several balls available for each group. One player bats, one fields the ball and returns it to the catcher, and the catcher replaces the ball on the batting tee.
3. Students rotate positions after every five hits.

FIGURE   6.4
Batting a Pitched Ball.

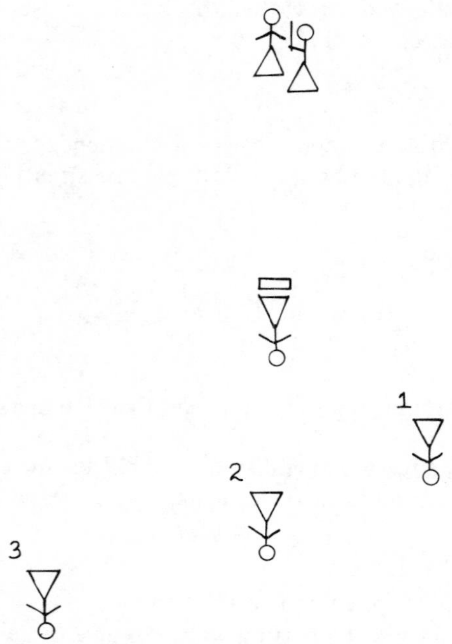

Batting a Pitched Ball (Figure 6.4)

1. Establish a line of direction for batted balls.
2. Position students in groups of six: three fielders, a pitcher, a catcher, and a batter.
3. Players rotate after each batter has hit five pitched balls. Fielder number 1 becomes the batter, the batter becomes the catcher, the catcher becomes the pitcher, the pitcher becomes fielder number 3, fielder number 3 becomes fielder number 2, and fielder number 2 becomes fielder number 1 (see figure 6.4).
4. Repeat until all players have made five hits.

Third Hit: Bat and Run (Figure 6.5)

1. Position eight players on a diamond for a regulation game. The ninth player is a permanent, skilled pitcher (perhaps the teacher).
2. One additional student bats at home plate.
3. The batter is allowed three hits.

FIGURE   6.5
Third Hit: Bat and Run.

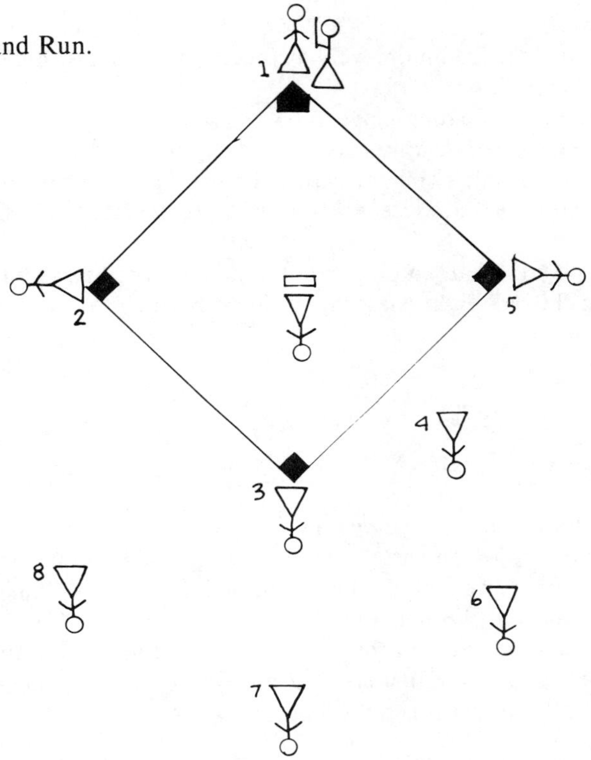

4. On the third hit, the batter runs the bases. The fielders play the ball, attempting to put the runner out.
5. After the batter is either out or crosses home plate, all players rotate. The batter moves to position 8, the catcher to batter, and all other players move one position number lower (see figure 6.5).

Fungo Hit and Field

1. Establish a line of direction for batted balls.
2. Position students in groups of three to six, including one batter and several fielders.
3. Batters practice hand/eye coordination by tossing a ball into the air and hitting it.
4. Fielders catch or field the ball and return it to the batter.
5. After the batter has hit ten balls, players rotate so all players eventually have a turn at bat.

Pepper Hit and Field

1. Arrange six to eight fielding players at three-foot intervals in a line ten to fifteen feet from a batter.
2. The batter faces the fielding players.
3. A ball is tossed by one fielding player to the batter.
4. The batter takes a half-swing, directing the ball back out toward the fielders. (Good concentration and eye contact with the ball enable the batter to contact the ball.)
5. The fielders play the ball and immediately toss it back to the hitter.
6. After hitting the ball eight consecutive times, rotate so all players eventually have a turn at bat.

Strategy

Mock Game Situations

1. Position a fielding team on a diamond.
2. The teacher acts as fungo batter and calls out game situations for the fielding team to visualize. For example, the teacher might call out, "One out, runner on second, where do you throw the ball?"
3. The teacher bats the ball and the fielders enact the mock situation.
4. After completing the play, fielders return the ball to the catcher at home plate. The teacher calls out another situation and play continues.

Variation

Add runners to each mock game situation. Each situation might be a continuation of the previous play so that the runners stay on base.

LEAD-UP GAMES

Tennis Softball (Grades 2–6)

This is a fun, recreational game played to teach the rules of softball.

Equipment

Tennis racket, five-inch playground ball, three bases, home plate

Procedures

1. Place one team in fielding position on a softball diamond and assign one team to bat.
2. Play regulation softball rules, substituting a tennis racket for a bat and a five-inch playground ball for the softball.

Variations

1. Speed up the game by allowing only two pitches and calling foul balls out.
2. Allow the entire offensive team to bat, and then change so the other team comes to bat. Count runs rather than outs during each team's turn at bat.

Hustle Ball (Grades 4–12)

This fast-moving game allows more players to participate and to practice base-running skills.

Equipment

Rubber volleyball, bat, three bases, home plate

Procedures

1. Select teams of nine to fifteen players. Designate the teacher or other leader as pitcher for both teams.
2. Position the catcher, pitcher, shortstop, and basemen on the diamond, with the remaining players scattered throughout the outfield.
3. Pitch a rubber volleyball or playground ball with an arch, like a slow-pitched softball.
4. Enforce regulation softball rules with the following exceptions:
    a. Don't call balls or strikes. Each batter must hit the ball on one of three allowed pitches.
    b. A player who swings and misses one time is out.
    c. A player who hits a foul ball is out.
    d. The team going in to bat has ten seconds to place a batter in position to hit. Failure to do so results in an out.

Fielders' Softball (Grades 4–12)

This game is designed to practice throwing, catching, and fielding skills.

Equipment

Three bases, home plate, bats, regulation softballs, gloves, chest protectors, face masks, backstop

Procedures

1. Assign nine players to a team.
2. Each player on the batting team takes a turn to hit before the team is retired to the field.
3. The batter must hit one of three balls pitched by the teacher or be called out.

4. Foul balls are counted as strikes. After three strikes, the batter is out, but the number of outs for the team is not recorded.
5. After a hit, the batter runs to each base and crosses home plate. The fielding team scores points in the following manner:
   a. The first player to field or catch the ball throws to a teammate. When the teammate catches the ball, a point is scored.
   b. A point is scored each time the ball is *caught* by a different player on the fielding team until the runner reaches home plate.
   c. If a fielder drops the ball, scoring ceases and the runner advances home.
   d. A fielding player may not catch the ball more than once until all team members have caught a ball.
   e. Should the base runner still be en route to home plate when everyone on the fielding team has caught the ball once, fielders may begin throwing and catching again.
   f. The runner may not interfere with a ball being thrown for a point. If the runner intentionally interferes, the fielding team scores three points and the runner returns to the end of the batting line.
6. After all players on the batting team have hit, the two teams change places.

Variations

1. Assign more players to a team.
2. Younger players continue throwing for points after dropping the ball. However, the fielding team scores no point unless they catch the ball.

Flag Softball (Grades 6–12)

This game emphasizes both hitting to place the ball and fielding.

Equipment

Three bases, home plate, bats, regulation softballs, gloves, chest protectors, face masks, backstop, eight flags

Procedures (Figure 6.6)

1. Teams consist of nine players, including the pitcher.
2. Flags are placed in the infield and outfield, outside of the base paths (see figure 6.6). Each flag is marked either 1, 2, 3, or HR (home run).

FIGURE   6.6
Flag Softball.

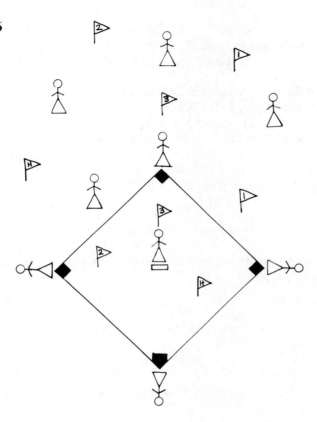

3. The batter attempts to hit the ball to a specific flag and then runs to the base that corresponds to the number on the flag.
4. All regulation softball rules apply as soon as the batter becomes a base runner.
5. A ball hit to the home run flag allows all players on base to proceed home free. A ball hit to any other flag leaves all base runners at risk.

Coed Softball (Grades 4–12)

Equipment

Three bases, home plate, bats, regulation softballs, gloves, chest protectors, face masks, backstop

Procedures

1. Play according to official softball rules.
2. Incorporate any of the following rule modifications to make play enjoyable and safe:
   a. At least four girls must be on the team (five when playing slow-pitch).
   b. Two girls must play in the infield.
   c. Alternate boys and girls when batting.
   d. When a boy walks, the next batter (a girl) may choose whether to walk or hit.
   e. Position both a boy and a girl on the pitcher's mound. The girl pitches to the girls and the boy to the boys.

Slow Pitch Softball (Grades 5–12)

This game allows players to participate in an official softball game without requiring players with fast pitch skills.

Equipment

Three bases, home plate, bats, regulation softballs, gloves, chest protectors, face masks, backstop

Procedures

1. Position two teams on a softball diamond, one team at bat and one team in the field.
2. Play official softball rules with the following exceptions:
   a. Teams consist of ten players. The extra player is an outfielder.
   b. The pitcher must deliver each pitch with a perceptible arc (one foot). The ball must reach a height of at least six feet from the ground but not exceed a maximum height of twelve feet from the ground. (Modify heights for young players.)
   c. The batter must take a full swing at the ball. A bunt or chop is illegal.
   d. A batter hit by a pitched ball is not entitled to take first base. The pitch that hits the batter is declared a ball.
   e. The pitcher may not pitch the ball behind the back or between the legs.
   f. A pitched ball that touches home plate is not a strike unless the batter swings at it.
   g. A base runner who leaves the base before the pitch crosses home plate is out.

Twelve-Player Softball (Grades 6–12)

This game is designed to give each participant an opportunity to play several different positions.

Equipment

Three bases, home plate, bats, regulation softballs, gloves, chest protectors, face masks, backstop

Procedures

1. Follow official softball rules.
2. At each diamond select four teams of three players each to cover each of the following positions:
   a. One team of three batters
   b. One team of pitcher, catcher, and shortstop
   c. One team of first, second, and third base players (infielders)
   d. One team of left, right, and center fielders (outfielders)
3. When the team at bat gets three outs, all teams rotate as follows:
   a. Batters to outfield
   b. Outfielders to infield
   c. Infielders to pitcher, catcher, and shortstop
   d. Pitcher, catcher, and shortstop to batters
4. Continue play until each team has had at least one turn at bat.

Work-ups (Grades 6–12)

This game allows players to practice softball skills while rotating to play all positions.

Equipment

Three bases, home plate, bats, regulation softballs, gloves, chest protectors, face masks, backstop

Procedures (Figure 6.7)

1. Play according to official softball rules.
2. Players consist of a catcher (number 1 in figure 6.7), pitcher (number 2), first baseman (number 3), right shortstop (number 4), second baseman (number 5), left shortstop (number 6), third baseman (number 7), left fielder (number 8), center fielder (number 9), right fielder (number 10), and four batters.

FIGURE   6.7
Work-ups.

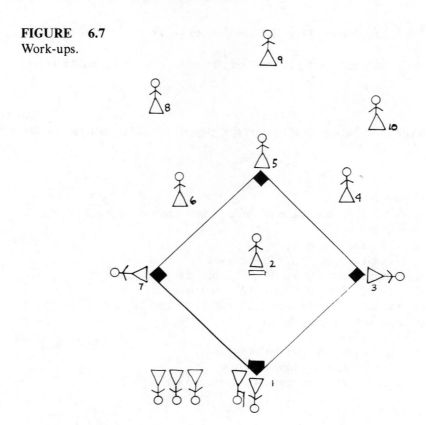

3. When a batting player is out, the fielding players rotate one numbered position lower, with the catcher moving to the number 4 batting position and the player who is out moving to the right fielder's (number 10) position.
4. If a fielder catches a fly ball, the fielder and the batter exchange positions. If the fielders perform a double play, all players rotate two numbered positions lower.

Variation

Rotate the batter to the outfield after five hits.

SKILL TESTS

Throw for Distance (Figure 6.8)

Mark the field at designated intervals. Place the first marker fifty feet from the starting line, the second seventy-five feet, and several subsequent markers every five yards. Mark a six- to ten-foot take-off area behind the restraining line. Provide a container of reg-

FIGURE   6.8
Throw for Distance.

FIGURE   6.9
Accuracy Throw for Distance.

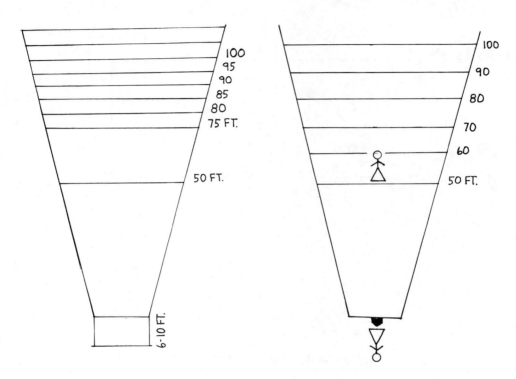

ulation softballs. Each student attempts three throws for distance from behind the restraining line. The student's score is the distance of the longest throw measured to the
nearest foot.

Accuracy Throw for Distance (Figure 6.9)

In the area between home plate and second base, mark the field in ten-foot intervals
starting fifty feet from home plate. Each student stands on the fifty-foot line and makes
three attempts to throw the ball to the catcher at home plate. Score the throw if the
catcher catches the ball with one or both feet on home plate. After each successful
attempt, the student moves back ten feet and repeats the process. The score is the
longest distance at which the student can throw with accuracy. Use regulation softballs.

FIGURE   6.10
Throw for Accuracy.

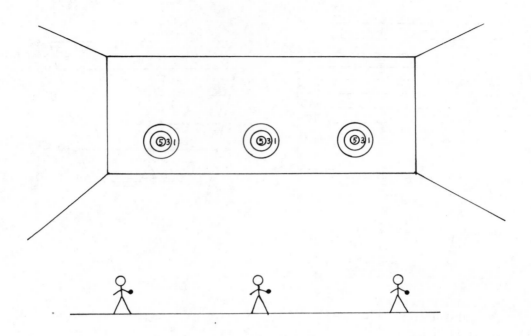

Throw for Accuracy (Figure 6.10)

Set up a throwing area by marking a restraining line forty feet from a wall target four-and-a-half feet above the floor. The target should contain three rings that are sixty, forty, and twenty inches in diameter. Each ring is worth one, three, or five points, respectively. Using a regulation softball, each student is allowed three attempts to hit the target. Balls that hit a line score the higher number of points. Total the points for each student's score.

Variation

Mark one circle, sixty inches in diameter, and score one point for each accurate throw.

Fielding Ground Balls

The teacher or aide stands at home plate with a container of regulation softballs, and the student stands approximately ten feet in front of second base. The teacher throws five ground balls to the student: two to each side of second base, not more than fifteen feet from the base, and one in front of the base. To score a point, the student must cleanly field the ball and throw it accurately to a player standing on either first or third base. Another student gathers fielded balls and returns them to the container at home plate.

Catching and Throwing Fly Balls

The teacher or aide stands at the pitcher's mound with a container of regulation balls, and the student stands in center field. The teacher throws three fly balls to the student. To score a point, the student must catch the fly ball and throw it accurately to a player standing on second base.

Catching

The teacher or aide stands at the shortstop position and the student stands at first base. The teacher throws three balls to the student. To score a point, the student must catch the ball.

Pitching

Each student pitches ten balls at a target (from a distance determined by the students' age and skill level). Students score one point for each legally pitched ball that hits the target, including any ball that hits the outer line on the target.

Batting

1. The teacher or aide pitches five balls. The student scores a point for each ball hit out of the infield.
2. Use a checklist to evaluate each student's batting technique in a game.

	YES	NO
Feet in stride position		
Hands together, left hand below right (if right-handed)		
Correct stance in relation to plate		
Elbows away from body		
Knees and hips flexed		
Bat up and off shoulder		
Parallel swing		
Weight shift to front foot		

Game Play

The teacher or aide tallies the following information for each student in a game situation:

NAME	BALLS CAUGHT	ERRORS	WALKS	STRIKE-OUTS	FLY OUTS	HITS			
						1B	2B	3B	HR

WRITTEN TEST

COMPLETION

1. The player positioned between second and third base is the _____ .
2. When a batter chalks up three strike pitches without making a safe hit, the pitcher earns a _____ .
3. A _____ is a hit ball caught by any player on the field before it touches the ground.
4. The playing area between first, second, and third bases and home is the _____ .
5. The type of pitch that requires one revolution of the arm is a _____ .
6. Remaining on base until after a fly ball is caught and then attempting to advance a base is called _____ .
7. A ball that hits inside the baseline but rolls out before being touched by any player is a _____ .
8. A half swing type of hit used to advance a player into possible scoring position is a _____ .
9. When a batter has taken three balls and two strikes, it is a _____ .
10. The area between the shoulders and knees of a batter is the _____ .
11. The base at which sliding is *not* permitted until after the base is touched by the runner is _____ .
12. The player who commits a passed ball is the _____ .

TRUE OR FALSE

T   F   13. An infield fly always results in an out regardless of whether the ball is caught.

T   F   14. The center fielder calls the fly balls for the outfield players.

T   F   15. The clean-up hitter is the fourth batter.

T   F   16. When the catcher catches a foul tip ball on the third strike, the batter is out.

T   F   17. A ball landing in the outfield and rolling into foul territory is a foul ball.

T   F   18. When fielding a ground ball, the fingers within the glove should be pointed upward.

MULTIPLE CHOICE

19. A bunt is always performed
    a. to advance a runner to scoring position.
    b. by the second player in the lineup.
    c. by the fastest player on the team.
    d. while standing in the batter's box.
20. Before releasing the ball, the pitcher must present the ball
    a. for thirty seconds.
    b. for three seconds.
    c. before stepping on the pitcher's plate.
    d. with one hand on the ball and the ball in the glove.
21. An inning is defined as
    a. each team committing three outs.
    b. scoring one run and committing three outs.
    c. completing two hits and three outs.
    d. none of the above.
22. The two teams do not play the bottom of the last inning when
    a. the home team is ahead by seven or more runs.
    b. darkness has descended.
    c. the home team is ahead.
    d. a player on the visiting team is cited for unsportsmanlike conduct.
23. A runner may leave the base
    a. as soon as the pitcher receives the ball.
    b. after the ball is hit.
    c. after the pitcher releases the ball.
    d. after the pitcher steps onto the pitcher's plate.
24. The runner is out
    a. when hit by a batted ball while running from first to second base.
    b. after dropping the bat in the batter's box.
    c. when touching the base another runner occupies.
    d. when running two feet outside the baseline.

DIAGRAM

Mark and name the positions of the players on a regulation team.

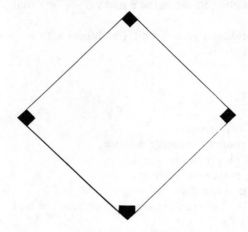

TEST KEY

COMPLETION

1. shortstop
2. strikeout
3. fly ball or fly out
4. diamond or infield

5. windmill
6. tagging up
7. foul ball
8. bunt

9. full count
10. strike zone
11. first base
12. catcher

TRUE OR FALSE

13. F
14. F
15. T
16. T
17. F
18. F

MULTIPLE CHOICE

19. d
20. b
21. a
22. c
23. c
24. a

CHAPTER SEVEN

TENNIS

Tennis is a game played by both young and old, male and female. It is a popular spectator sport worldwide.

EQUIPMENT

Tennis balls
Fleeceballs (for gymnasium play)
Rackets
Nets/Court

SUGGESTIONS FOR INSTRUCTIONAL PROFICIENCY

Tennis is a sport that requires precision in performing basic strokes. Therefore, students must spend considerable time developing precise skill execution. Often devices such as a ball-throwing machine, a suspended ball, a bounce-back net, or hanging nets can alleviate player frustration and aid in skill development.

1. Provide each player with a racket.
2. Supply a container of balls for each court.
3. Check courts daily for unsafe conditions. Keep cleaning and drying equipment close to courts. Wet courts cause ball damage.
4. Inspect for damaged equipment regularly. Replace and repair broken rackets as needed.
5. Penalize students who jump over the net.
6. Establish a line of direction and provide adequate space for practice, especially during indoor play.
7. Expect students to retrieve balls that are hit out of play. Incorporate a reliable system of accountability.
8. Teach rules, strategy, and court etiquette along with skills.
9. Introduce the regulation game when students can rally the ball.
10. Allow students experience in singles and doubles play. Change partners often.
11. Provide time to discuss care and purchase of equipment.

TEACHING THE BASICS

The following progression is suggested:

1. **Preliminary Actions**

    Grip
      Forehand
      Backhand
    Conditioning, hand-eye coordination: Using a forehand grip, student
      continuously hits the ball in the air or to the ground. Ball may rebound
      from racket edge or face.

2. **Stroke Practice**

    Forehand and backhand
      Ready position
      Footwork: Teach basic body shift from a stationary position. Add
      movement on the court as students gain proficiency.
    Serve
      Flat
      Spin
    Volley

3. **Regulation Court Play**

    Court coverage
      Offense
      Defense
    Court play
      Scoring (include tie-breakers)
      Rules and terminology
    Strategy
      Singles
      Doubles

4. **Advanced Strokes**

    Lob
    Smash

DRILLS

Forehand and Backhand

Forehand/Backhand Triad (Figures 7.1 and 7.2)

1. Arrange players in groups of three. One player hits, one tosses, and one retrieves.
2. The hitter stands at the baseline. The tosser stands midcourt, six to eight feet to the side of the hitter. (For the forehand swing, the tosser stands diagonally across from the player's racket side, as in figure 7.1. For the backhand swing, the tosser stands diagonally from the player's backhand side, as shown in figure 7.2.) The retriever stands across the net in backcourt.
3. The tosser tosses the ball underhand, aiming diagonally to the side and in front of the hitter.

FIGURE   7.1
Forehand Triad.

FIGURE   7.2
Backhand Triad.

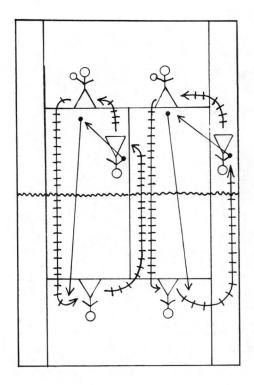

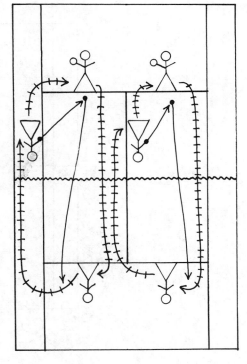

4. The hitter hits the ball across the net and the retriever returns it.
5. After the hitter hits ten balls, players rotate. The hitter becomes the retriever, the retriever becomes the tosser, and the tosser becomes the hitter.
6. When the hitter develops proficiency, advance to hitting a bounced ball.

Forehand/Backhand Teacher Toss and Hit (Figure 7.3)

1. The teacher stands at midnet with fifty to a hundred balls.
2. Five to ten players stand in single file at the baseline. Three additional players retrieve balls at the opposite end of the court.
3. The teacher tosses balls to the hitters. Each player in turn hits several forehand strokes and then moves to the retrieving line on the opposite side of the court.
4. Players rotate, bringing the retrievers into the hitting line. New hitters repeat the process.
5. Repeat the stroking process using the backhand.

FIGURE   7.3
Forehand/Backhand
Teacher Toss and Hit.

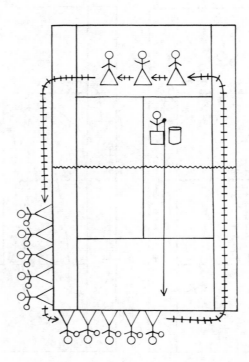

Variation

The teacher moves to backcourt and strokes the ball to players in line.

Forehand/Backhand Controlled Basics (Figure 7.4)

1. Position partners on a court facing each other across the net.
2. In each pair, one player, the tosser, stands close to the net. The hitter faces the tosser four to five feet from the opposite side of the net. Provide extra balls for the tossers.
3. The tosser sends the ball over the net with an underhand toss. The hitter returns the ball, aiming at the hand of the tosser with a gentle, controlled hit.
4. The hitter takes one step back after mastering stroke placement from the first distance.
5. Players switch roles when the hitter is able to hit from the baseline, or after ten to twenty hits.

FIGURE   7.4
Forehand/Backhand
Controlled Basics.

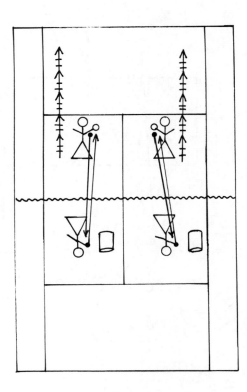

Forehand/Backhand Crosscourt or Down the Line (Figure 7.5)

1. Position six to eight players side by side along one baseline.
2. Two experienced hitters stand at mid-serve court on the opposite side of the net with fifty to a hundred balls.
3. Hitters alternately toss the ball to a receiver, identifying the receiver by name, and request ball return of down-the-line or crosscourt.
4. The receiver moves from the baseline to return the ball as requested.
5. After completing the shot, the receiver moves back into line and the hitters call another name.
6. When the receivers complete a designated number of turns, the ball is put into play off the hitter's racket.

FIGURE   7.5
Forehand/Backhand
Crosscourt or Down the
Line.

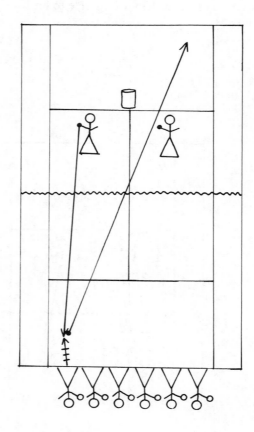

Forehand/Backhand Self-Hit

1. Individual players drop the ball and stroke it (courtesy stroke) into a net, fence, wall, or backboard.
2. Beginning players catch the ball after each hit and repeat the action.
3. When players achieve proficiency, they hit the ball continuously rather than catching and serving again.

Variation (Figure 7.6)

Players stroke the ball into a target, for example, a net line, rectangle, or circle drawn on a fence or wall.

FIGURE   7.6
Variation on the Forehand/Backhand Self-Hit.

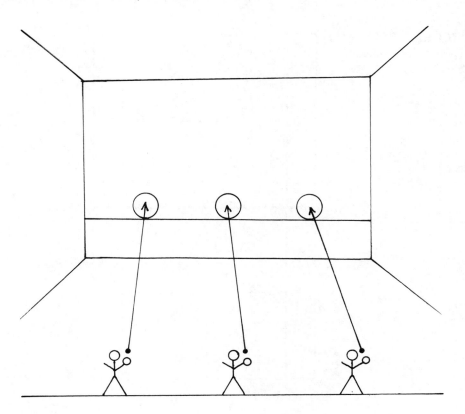

Forehand/Backhand Service Court Play (Figure 7.7)

1. Assign groups of four, with two players on each court behind the service line.
2. Any player may initiate play with a courtesy stroke.
3. Players are expected to exercise ball control as they stroke the ball to land within the service court and the alleys.
4. The ball is hit once on each side of the net.
5. When an error occurs, the ball is put back in play by the nearest participant.
6. Players move to one-on-one practice when they can control play. In the one-on-one drill, one twosome strokes back and forth on the left side of the court and the other twosome on the right side.

Variation

Players with sufficient skill execute the drill from baseline positions to rally the full court.

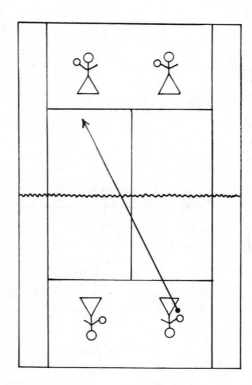

FIGURE   7.7
Forehand/Backhand
Service Court Play.

Skilled Forehand/Backhand Shuttle (Figure 7.8)

1. Assign six players to a shuttle line on each side of the net behind the baseline.
2. The first player in one line puts the ball in play with a courtesy stroke, then runs to the end of the opposite line.
3. The receiver returns the ball with either a forehand or backhand, then runs to the end of the opposite line.
4. Each time someone makes an error, a player in the line that has the ball puts the ball back in play.
5. Play continues until players hit consistently.

FIGURE   7.8
Skilled Forehand/Backhand Shuttle.

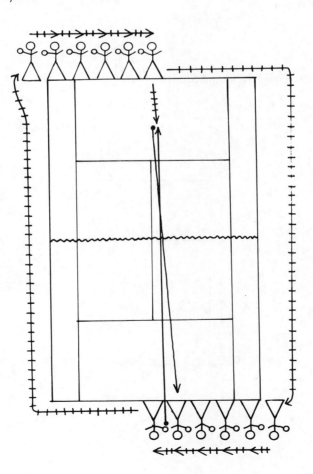

Variation

Players making two mistakes—hitting the ball into the net or out of bounds, or missing the ball entirely—are eliminated. When only one player with less than two errors remains, players return to original positions to begin again.

Four-Player Forehand/Backhand Shuttle (Figure 7.9)

1. Position four players on the court, two in each alley.
2. Two additional players are positioned at the net on each side of the court.
3. Player A (see figure 7.9) hits down the line to the backhand of player B.
4. Player B hits crosscourt to the backhand of player C.
5. Player C hits down the line to the forehand of player D.
6. Player D hits crosscourt to the forehand of player A, who starts play again.
7. Any player who commits an error exchanges places with one of the extra players at the net.

FIGURE   7.9
Four-Player Forehand/Backhand Shuttle.

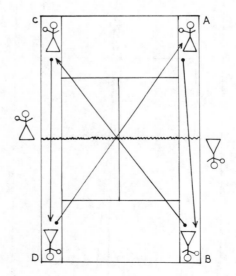

Serve

Throw Serve (Figure 7.10)

1. Position two file lines of three players on each side of the net behind the baseline (or behind the service line for beginners).
2. The first player in each line on one side of the net throws three overhand balls diagonally across the net and into the service court, using a baseball motion. The thrower then moves to the end of the line.
3. The players on the opposite side of the net return thrown balls to a container.
4. When the "servers" have thrown fifty to a hundred balls, the retrievers return the balls using the same throwing procedure, and the former throwers become retrievers.

FIGURE   7.10
Throw Serve.

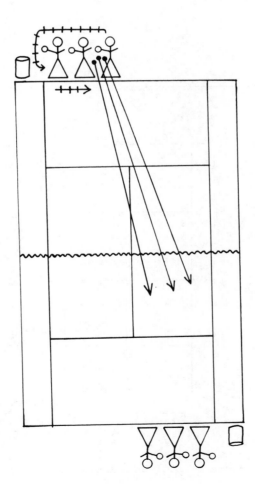

Fence Serve (Figure 7.11)

1. Position the entire class facing a protective fence. Students should be six to ten feet from the fence and six to eight feet apart from each other.
2. Players serve into the fence.
3. The instructor moves around to give feedback to each player.

Court Serve (Figure 7.12)

1. Position four players on each half-court. Set fifty to a hundred balls in a container on the servers' side.
2. On the servers' side of the net, two of the servers practice serving from right court to right court. The other two serve from left court to left court, alternating with the right-court servers.

FIGURE   7.11
Fence Serve.

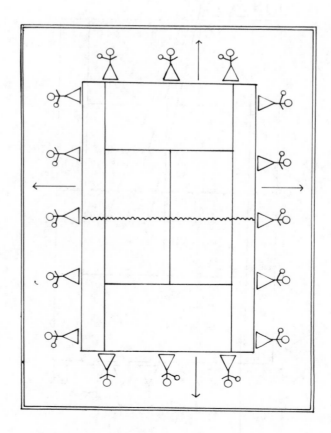

3. On the opposite side of the court, the other four players retrieve the balls and place them in a container.
4. When the servers have used all the balls, the retrievers exchange roles with the servers and practice begins again.

Court Serve and Return (Figure 7.13)

1. Position four players on the court with two on each side of the net.
2. Each player, in turn, attempts ten serves. The receiving players return every legal serve.
3. Servers allow the returned ball to land without further play.
4. After all players have served, the players on each side of the net exchange service courts and play begins again.

FIGURE   7.12
Court Serve.

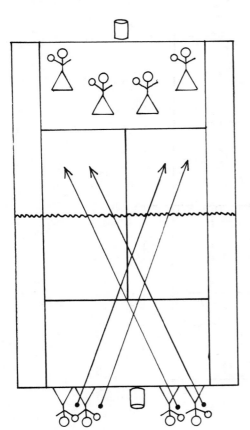

FIGURE   7.13
Court Serve and Return.

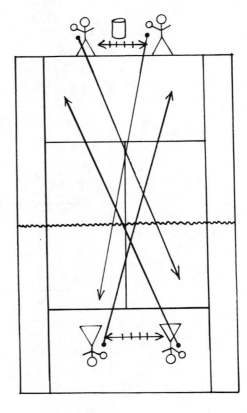

Number Serve (Figure 7.14)

1. Position two servers and two retrievers on each court. Provide fifty to a hundred balls for the servers.
2. The servers serve the ball diagonally across the net deep into the numbered areas of the service court.
3. Players serve three balls to the retriever's forehand (areas 1 and 3 on figure 7.14) and then three balls to the retriever's backhand (areas 2 and 4).
4. Players switch service courts after three hits, and the process is repeated.
5. When all the served balls have been returned to a container, retrievers and servers exchange positions.

Variation

Retrievers become receivers and each serve is returned with a ground stroke.

FIGURE 7.14
Number Serve.

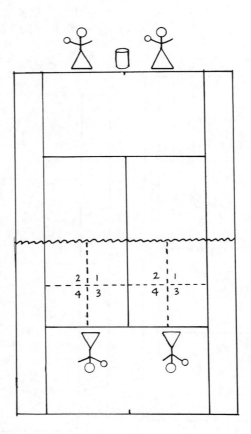

Volley

Catch Volley

1. Space five throwers evenly along the court, each facing a partner across the net. Partners stand three to four feet from the net.
2. Each thrower tosses the ball underhand to a partner, aiming at shoulder height for either a forehand or backhand return.
3. Each catcher steps and reaches forward with the racket hand to catch the ball in the appropriate position for either a forehand or backhand volley. The catcher then becomes the thrower and repeats the procedure.

Racket Toss Volley

1. Two players face partners across the net. Hitters stand three to four feet from the net and tossers stand close to the service line.
2. Tossers gently throw the ball overhand and chest high to the hitter's forehand position. The hitter then returns the ball with a volley to the tosser.
3. Tossers throw five balls to the hitter's forehand and five to the backhand. Then partners reverse roles.

Variation

Vary the height and position of the ball toss. Mix up forehand and backhand tosses so the receiver cannot anticipate ball placement.

Racket Hit Volley (Figure 7.15)

1. Position three hitters in a file line behind one baseline and three retrievers on the opposite side of the net with fifty to a hundred balls.
2. The first hitter moves to a volley position at the net.
3. The instructor or an experienced player strokes the ball from the service line to the player in volley position.
4. The hitter returns five forehand and five backhand volleys, then moves to the end of the line.
5. When the three hitters have volleyed all the balls, retrievers and hitters change places and play begins again.

Variation

The instructor or experienced player moves to the baseline to stroke the ball, varying the speed and direction of the stroke.

FIGURE   7.15
Racquet Hit Volley.

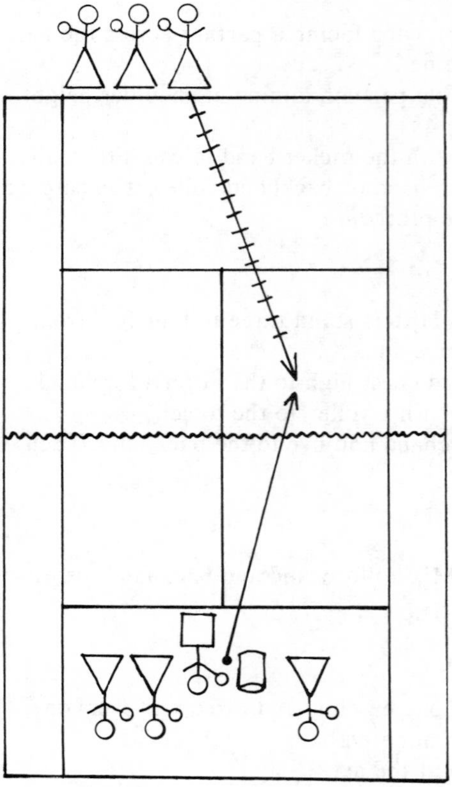

FIGURE   7.16
Triad Volley.

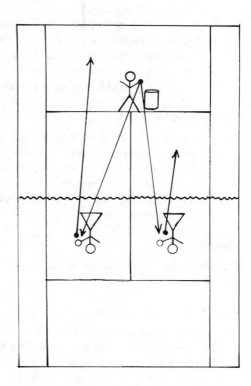

Triad Volley (Figure 7.16)

1. Assign threesomes. Two players stand three to five feet from the net. The third player is on the opposite side at the service line.
2. The lone player tosses the ball alternately to the opposite twosome, who volley the ball back.
3. Players rotate positions after the twosome have hit about fifty balls.
4. When receivers are able to consistently return easy-to-hit volleys, increase the speed of the toss and vary its direction.
5. When the receivers are able to return a variety of tosses with ease, the lone third player hits the ball off the racket rather than throwing it.

Partner Volley (Figure 7.17)

1. Assign four players to each court: two players at the net and two at the opposite baseline. The players facing each other are partners.

FIGURE   7.17
Partner Volley.

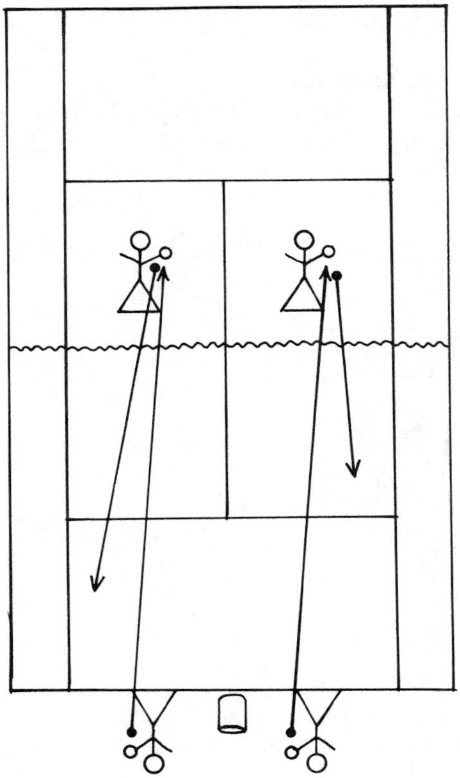

FIGURE   7.18
Toss Lob.

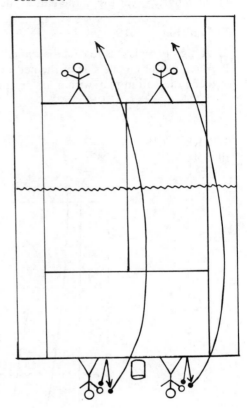

2. Each baseline player hits the ball over the net. The net player returns the ball with a volley.
3. After each net player hits ten forehand or backhand volleys, net and baseline players change places and play begins again.

Lob

Toss Lob (Figure 7.18)

1. Assign four players to each court: two players at the baseline, with fifty to a hundred balls, and two at the opposite midcourt. Partners face each other.
2. Each baseline player drops the ball and lobs it over the head of the midcourt partner.
3. After each baseline player hits ten lobs, partners change places and play begins again.

Variation

The midcourt player tosses the ball to the baseline player for the lob.

Hit Lob (Figure 7.19)

1. Assign two players to each baseline. Partners face each other.
2. Each player on one side of the net hits to the opposite baseline player. Players keep the ball in play with a lob or, if necessary, with a ground stroke.

FIGURE   7.19
Hit Lob.

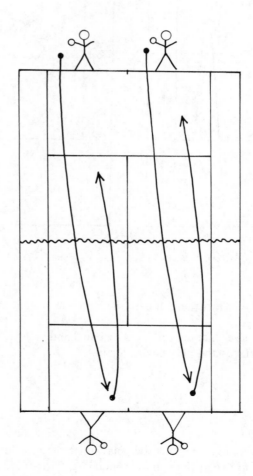

Smash

Partner Smash (Figure 7.20)

1. Assign four players to each court: two players at the baseline and two at the opposite midcourt. Partners face each other.
2. Each baseline player either tosses or hits a lob high to the midcourt partner. The midcourt partner moves to smash the ball.
3. After each midcourt player smashes ten balls, partners change places and play begins again.

FIGURE   7.20
Partner Smash.

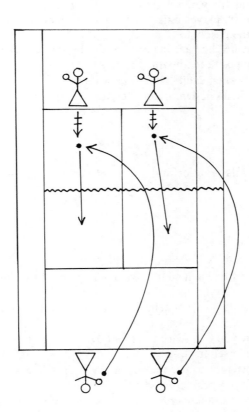

LEAD-UP GAMES

Deep Ball

This game is designed to allow students to practice hitting deep consistently.

Equipment

Court, rackets, balls

Procedures

1. Assign four players per court for a game.
2. One partner begins the game with a drop hit serve.
3. After the serve, each player must hit the ball deep enough to land between the service line and the baseline.
4. Balls landing outside the baseline and inside the service area are considered out of bounds. The opposite team wins the serve.
5. Service rotates between each of the four players.
6. The game ends when one team scores eleven points.

Net Control

This game gives students practice in gaining net position during doubles play.

Equipment

Court, rackets, balls

Procedures

1. Station four players on each court, two at the net and two behind the opposite baseline.
2. The instructor stands between courts and tosses a ball alternately to the baseline players.
3. The baseline players try to score the point even though they are disadvantaged by starting at the baseline.
4. The net players attempt to put the ball away with volleys or smashes while trying to maintain net position.
5. Play continues until all teams have had the opportunity to play at the net several times.

File Line Tennis

This fun game is designed to involve many people.

Equipment
Court, rackets, balls

Procedures
1. Ten players assume file line position at the baseline. The first player holds a racket.
2. Two students take positions on the opposite court, each with a racket. These students take turns drop serving the ball to the other court beyond the service line.
3. The first file line player returns the ball, quickly gives the racket to the next player in line, and then runs to the end of the file line. Each player repeats the pattern.
4. The twosome on the opposite court try to keep the ball in play, gradually increasing the level of difficulty as required.

Single-Doubles

This game challenges the advanced player and gives the less-skilled player doubles game practice.

Equipment
Court, rackets, balls

Procedures
1. Assign a doubles team and a single player to each court.
2. The doubles team will play doubles rules on one side of the court, and the single player will play singles rules on the other side of the court.
3. Follow regulation tennis rules for scoring and completing games.

Serve Master

Students play this game to perfect their serves.

Equipment
Court, rackets, balls

Procedures

1. Position two doubles teams on the court.
2. The player in the right service court begins play with a serve. This player continues to serve, rotating service courts, until a double fault occurs.
3. The players on the opposite side of the court return the balls after each serve.
4. Each legal serve counts one point.
5. After all players serve, the winner is the player with the highest number of points.

SKILL TESTS

Forehand/Backhand Court Placement (Figure 7.21)

The performer stands on the baseline to drop hit twenty balls into marked scoring areas in the singles court (ten forehand and ten backhand). Balls landing in the service area count two points. Balls landing beyond the service court count four points, and balls landing in the backcourt corners (marked four feet wide) count six points. When a ball lands on a line, count the higher value.

FIGURE   7.21
Forehand/Backhand
Court Placement.

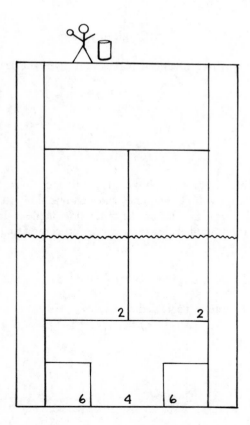

Backboard Rally

The performer faces a backboard behind a restraining line twenty-five feet from the wall. The student puts the ball in play with a drop hit and continues to hit it against the wall. The player may hit or volley the ball after any number of bounces. The player may cross the restraining line to retrieve or hit balls, but hits made from this area are not scored. An assistant stands out of the playing area, on the forehand side, to give balls to the hitter as needed. The student's score is the total number of balls hit against the wall from behind the restraining line in thirty seconds. Give each student three thirty-second trials.

As an alternative, mark a net line on the wall. Count only the hits that strike the wall on or above the line.

Serve Test (Figure 7.22)

The server hits ten balls to each service court. The student scores one point for each ball that lands in the correct service court but not in a marked corner section. Balls landing in the two-foot wide corner areas count three points. Record the total number of points for each student's score.

FIGURE   7.22
Serve Test.

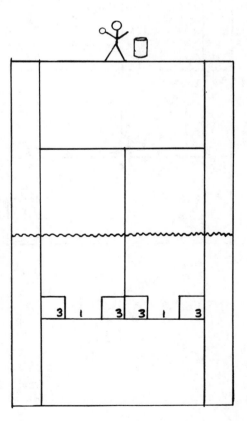

Volley Test (Figure 7.23)

The performer stands three to six feet from the net to receive a self-hit ground stroke from a player in the opposite court. The hitter hits ten balls to the performer's forehand and ten to the backhand. The performer must return each hit with a volley. Divide the court into sections for scoring purposes. Balls hit within the service courts score two points. Balls hit beyond the service line count four points. Balls hit within the lines that run parallel with each alley count three points in the service area and five points beyond the service area. Any ball that strikes a line scores the higher point value. The student's score is the total number of points earned.

FIGURE   7.23
Volley Test.

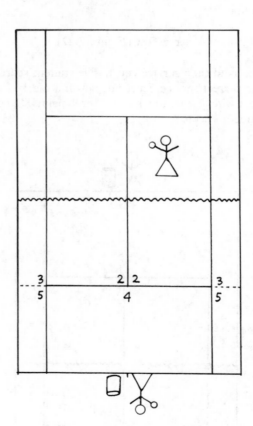

Performance Checklist

During a game, observe each player and award one to five points for correct skill execution (the better the execution, the higher the number of points).

SKILL	EVALUATION
Forehand/Backhand	
Ready position	
Move and stop before stroke	
Backswing	
Contact	
Followthrough	
Placement	
Serve	
Full arm motion	
Ball toss	
Speed	
Volley	
Ready position	
Footwork	
Contact	

WRITTEN TEST

TRUE OR FALSE

T   F   1. The same player serves throughout a game.

T   F   2. Line balls are considered good.

T   F   3. The service line on a tennis court is the one directly behind which the player must stand to serve.

T   F   4. A let serve allows the server another serve.

T   F   5. The service court is the same in a singles game as in a doubles game.

T   F   6. The playing court is the same in a singles game as in a doubles game.

T   F   7. The tennis net is the same height in the center as at the posts.

T   F   8. An underhand serve is a legal serve.

T   F   9. A player may hit the ball with two hands on the racket.

SCORING

Write the score for each play. Be sure you write the server's score first.

10. Server wins the point after deuce. _____
11. Receiver wins point after advantage out. _____
12. Server has one point, receiver has two. _____
13. Server has three points and the receiver has three points. _____
14. Server has three points and the receiver has zero. _____
15. Receiver wins point after advantage in. _____

TEST KEY

TRUE OR FALSE

1. T	4. T	7. F
2. T	5. T	8. T
3. F	6. F	9. T

SCORING

10. Adv. in
11. Game
12. 15–30
13. Deuce
14. 40–Love
15. Deuce

CHAPTER EIGHT

TRACK AND FIELD

Track and field activities form the basis for all sports skills. Most students have the aptitude to become proficient in at least one track and field event. The following activities are designed to encourage participation, honest effort, and skillful performance.

EQUIPMENT

Oval track and field facility
    Long jump landing pit, rake
    High jump landing pit, standards, crossbar or elastic
Finish yarn
.22-caliber starting gun, blanks
Stopwatches
Measuring tapes
Relay batons
Tickets for participation and performance
Clipboards, paper, pencils

SUGGESTIONS FOR INSTRUCTIONAL PROFICIENCY

1. Condition students for these skills with daily jogging and stretching activities. Do so well in advance of the instructional unit. (Short periods of exercise are all that is necessary.)
2. Teach each of the skills necessary to participate in the drill ticket procedure.
3. Provide practice time and analysis before using the ticket program.
4. Use easy-breaking finish yarn. This will eliminate skin burns if someone fails to drop the finish tape at the appropriate time.

TEACHING THE BASICS

The following progression is suggested:

1. **Sprint**

   Starting position
   Acceleration
   Running form
   Finish form

2. **Shuttle Relay**

   Running with baton
   Baton hand-off

3. **Standing Long Jump**

   Starting position
   Landing position

4. **Running Long Jump**

   Approach (run-up)
   Take-off
   Flight
   Landing position

5. **High Jump**

   (Teach flop or straddle roll only if a safe, soft landing pit is available.)
   Approach (run-up)
   Take-off
   Flight
   Landing position

PRACTICE SESSIONS

Use a ticket program to help motivate students to participate and also to evaluate their performance in all events. Each time a student participates in any event, issue a colored ticket to that person with the event stamped or printed on it. At the end of the unit, collect all tickets to evaluate student participation and performance (suggestions for scoring tickets appear later in this chapter). This system will encourage students to participate and to work for excellence as each student earns a tangible reward for each performance.

Teach and practice track and field skills over a two- or three-week period of time, using the ticket procedure as a motivational practice system.

Track Tickets

Cut colored three-by-five-inch index cards into one-inch strips and stamp or print the name of a specific event on each. Color-code the tickets for level of performance. The following examples demonstrate some of the qualifying levels that could be set in several specific events for junior high or middle school students.

Dashes and Relays

Blue   = First place
Red   = Second place
White   = Third place
Yellow = Fourth place

High Jump

Blue   = 3'9'' or higher
Red   = 3'6''–3'9''
White   = 3'3''–3'6''
Yellow = 3'0''–3'3''
Green   = 2'9''–3'0''
Orange = 2'6''–2'9''

Running Long Jump

Blue   = 11' or longer
Red   = 10'–11'
White   = 9'–10'
Yellow = 8'6''–9'
Green   = 8'0''–8'6''
Orange = 6'–8'

Standing Long Jump

Blue   = 70″ and longer
Red   = 65″–70″
White = 60″–65″
Yellow = 55″–60″
Green = 50″–55″
Orange = 40″–50″

PROCEDURES

Dashes

Run four students at a time in the dashes. Give the first place finisher a blue ticket, the second place a red, third a white, and fourth a yellow. After running, the students form a line with others who received the same color ticket. After every student has run once, those who received the same color ticket in their first race run against each other four at a time. For example, all those who received a white ticket in their first race run against each other so that the next time some earn blue tickets, some red, and some yellow. Repeat this procedure until students have run the desired number of races. You may time runners with stopwatches or simply give them tickets for the order they finished.

It is helpful to arrange the tickets in packets so that they are in the order they will be awarded—that is, one blue, one red, one white, and one yellow in each packet.

The 440-Yard (Meter) Relay

Divide the class into teams of four. Select four teams to compete. Award tickets according to the order teams finish in or in keeping with times recorded on a stopwatch.

Since there are four people on each relay team, it is helpful to arrange the tickets in packets in the following order: four blues, four reds, four whites, and four yellows. Hand out the four tickets for each team after the last runner on each team crosses the finish line. The last runner then takes the responsibility of distributing the tickets to the other members of the team.

Jumping or Throwing

Each time a student participates in any event, give a colored ticket to that student according to the distance or height of the jump or throw. In the high jump, the student must legally clear the bar to get a ticket. In the long jump or in throwing events, the participant must perform a legal jump or throw (no scratches) to get a ticket. It is wise to set a minimum distance students must achieve; this encourages honest effort.

Field Events

It is best to keep tickets for each field event separated by color. At the end of the student's attempt, issue a colored ticket to match performance. Standards required for each color ticket in each event may vary depending on the student's grade level and the equipment and facilities available.

Scoring System

At the end of the unit, give each student a scoring sheet. Ask students to figure their total scores and to attach their tickets to the sheet. Score tickets as follows:

Eleven points for each ticket handed in
Three additional points for each blue ticket
Two additional points for each red ticket
One additional point for each white ticket

Use the total scores as you see fit to evaluate the student's performance. For example, arrange total scores in a distribution and then assign letter grades accordingly.

Jogging Program

You may use the same ticket system to conduct a jogging or running program. Each time a student runs a lap around the track, issue a lap ticket. Stamp these lap tickets with any appropriate name—for example, "Lap Ticket" or "Hares." At the end of the unit, students return their lap tickets to aid in evaluating student performance.

Additional Hints

1. Spend several days introducing the unit and teaching the skills involved in each event. After students have had this initial practice, begin awarding tickets for performance practice.
2. It is advisable to have the students write their names in ink on each of their tickets as soon as they return to the locker room after each class. Stress the students' responsibility for keeping track of their own tickets so they will not be misplaced, lost, or stolen.
3. Cutting and stamping these tickets takes a considerable amount of time. For example, if you have 300 students per day and each student hands in an average of 25 tickets in a five-week period of time, you are dealing with a total of 7,500 tickets. Therefore, it is best to start cutting and stamping tickets weeks in advance of the track and field unit rather than leaving it all until the night

before the events begin. Any method you can devise to cut down this time is extremely helpful. Perhaps the tickets could be printed instead of hand-stamped or ditto masters could be made to eliminate the stamping.

4. If you substitute some other material for index cards, keep the following in mind:

    a. The tickets must be of heavy enough construction that they will not easily tear or rumple.

    b. The tickets must be small enough to fit in a student's gym suit pocket so they won't get lost during the class period. Then students can keep them in their gym baskets or lockers until they are turned in at the end of the unit. However, some students prefer to keep their tickets at home so they won't be a temptation to other students.

WRITTEN TEST

TRUE OR FALSE

T F   1. Runners in a fifty-yard dash must remain in the same lane for the entire race.

T F   2. A runner should always run through the finish line.

T F   3. The Fosbury Flop is a long jump technique.

T F   4. A standing long jumper should be able to jump as far as a running long jumper.

T F   5. To run a lap means to run once around the track.

T F   6. A dash is considered an aerobic exercise.

T F   7. Running continuously for fifteen minutes at a time is an example of exercising aerobically.

T F   8. The scissors high jump requires the jumper to land on the back.

T F   9. After the hand-off, relay runners must remain in their own lanes until all other runners have passed them.

T F 10. A runner who drops the relay baton is disqualified from the race.

T F 11. Each high jumper has three trials to jump over the crossbar before it is moved up.

T F 12. The distance of a running long jump is measured from the front of the take-off board to a break in the landing pit sand.

T F 13. A legal standing long jump requires that both feet leave the ground at the same time.

T F 14. It is illegal to touch the high-jump bar with any part of the body even if the crossbar is not knocked off the standard.

T F 15. If a standing long jumper falls back and touches the hands on the ground behind the feet, the jump is measured from where the feet land.

T   F   16. Running outside one's lane can disqualify a relay runner.

T   F   17. The starting signal "take your marks, get set, go" is always used no matter how long the race.

T   F   18. A running long jumper is disqualified for falling to the side after touching the sand.

T   F   19. Touching one's foot beyond the take-off board constitutes an illegal long jump.

T   F   20. A runner is disqualified for running before the "go" signal.

TEST KEY

1. T	6. F	11. T	16. T
2. T	7. F	12. T	17. F
3. F	8. F	13. T	18. F
4. F	9. T	14. F	19. T
5. T	10. F	15. F	20. F

CHAPTER NINE

VOLLEYBALL

Volleyball is popular worldwide. The rules are easily adapted to a variety of facilities, equipment, coeducational activities, and team sizes.

EQUIPMENT

Nets/standards
Volleyballs or suitable substitutes (for example, Nerf balls or beach balls)

SUGGESTIONS FOR INSTRUCTIONAL PROFICIENCY

1. Provide one ball per person, or at least one ball for every four people. Official-size leather balls are recommended.
2. Substitute Nerf balls or beach balls of similar size when instructing beginning players.
3. Require students to care for equipment. Do not permit them to kick or sit on balls.
4. Teach the volley and pass without nets to allow more practice space.
5. Use wall space to teach skills such as the volley, the serve, the pass, and the spike. Mark a net-height line on the wall to practice these skills. (Using wall space is less gamelike but often necessary because of space constraints and skill levels.)
6. Arrange students so they practice in the same direction with sufficient space between them.
7. Stress ball control and high sets. Position students so the instructor can readily detect and correct errors.
8. Teach volleyball rules along with the skills.
9. Adapt the court size and the height of the net for elementary school children.

TEACHING THE BASICS

The following progression is suggested:

1. **Overhead Volley:** You may wish to teach the volley and forearm pass together.
2. **Forearm Pass:** Students must develop passing skills to be effective in returning the serve or other hard-hit balls.

3. **Serve:** Students must be able to serve before the class can play an official game.

   Underhand—Grades 5–12
   Overhead—Grades 7–12

4. **Set:** The set is an essential part of effective teamwork. Practice this skill with the net when possible.

   Front
   Back

5. **Hit (Spike):** Don't wait for students to perfect other skills before introducing this skill.
6. **Dig (One-Arm Pass):** Teach rolls and dives in conjunction with this skill.
7. **Strategy and Court Play**

DRILLS

Overhead Volley and Forearm Pass

Most of the following drills can be used for either the volley or the pass.

Toss Volley/Pass (Figure 9.1)

1. A skilled tosser stands five to eight feet from a line of receivers and throws the ball to the player on the far left.
2. The receiver volleys or passes the ball back to the tosser.
3. The tosser continues to toss the ball to each succeeding player. Each player in turn volleys or passes the ball back.
4. Practice continues in this manner until students demonstrate skill.

Self-Volley (Figure 9.2)

1. Students toss the balls high in the air and volley to themselves one to two feet above their heads.

FIGURE   9.1
Toss Volley/Pass.

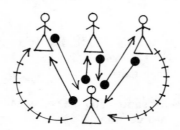

FIGURE 9.2
Self-Volley.

FIGURE 9.3
Partner Volley/Pass.

FIGURE 9.4
Wall Volley/Pass.

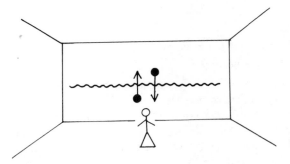

2. Gradually increase the height of the volley until it rises at least eight feet above the net.
3. Challenge students by increasing the number of required volleys from five to ten to fifteen or twenty.

Partner Volley/Pass (Figure 9.3)

1. Partners face each other, approximately four to eight feet apart.
2. One player tosses the ball to the other.
3. Partners volley or pass back and forth, keeping the ball above net height.

Wall Volley/Pass (Figure 9.4)

1. Mark a net-high line on the wall. Players stand three to six feet from the wall, with enough room between players to move side to side.
2. Each player tosses the ball up in the air and volleys or passes it above the wall line.
3. Steadily increase the number of volleys required and the height of the volley.

FIGURE   9.5
Line Volley/Pass.

FIGURE   9.6
File Line Volley/Pass.

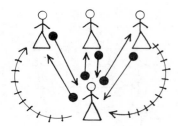

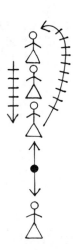

Line Volley/Pass (Figure 9.5)

1. One player, acting as leader, stands with the ball four to six feet in front of a line of players. These players stand side by side at three-foot intervals.
2. The leader volleys or passes the ball to each player in turn, making sure the ball is net-high or above.
3. Each player volleys or passes the ball back to the leader.
4. When all players have volleyed or passed, the leader moves to the end of the line and a new leader rotates from the opposite end of the line.

File Line Volley/Pass (Figure 9.6)

1. A leader stands with the ball four to six feet in front of a file line.
2. The leader volleys or passes the ball, at net height or above, to each player in turn.
3. Each player volleys or passes the ball back to the leader and then moves to the end of the line.
4. When each player has volleyed or passed the ball, the leader rotates to the end of the line. The first player in the file line then becomes the leader.

Shuttle Volley/Pass (Figure 9.7)

1. Players in two file lines face each other from a distance of five to eight feet.
2. One of the first players in line begins play by volleying or passing the ball *high* to the first player in the opposite line, then moving to the end of the same line.

FIGURE   9.7
Shuttle Volley/Pass.

FIGURE   9.8
Shuttle Wall Volley/Pass.

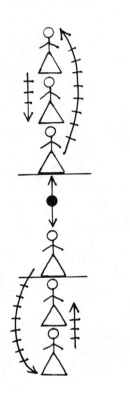

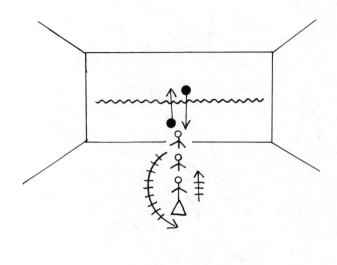

3. The receiver volleys the ball back, and the process continues until all players have volleyed or until a player drops the ball.

Shuttle Wall Volley/Pass (Figure 9.8)

1. Players in a file line face a wall five to eight feet away.
2. The first player in line puts the ball in play against the wall.
3. Each player in line volleys or passes the ball against the wall and moves to the end of the line.
4. This process continues until all players have volleyed or passed a designated number of times or until a player drops the ball.

FIGURE 9.9
Circle Volley/Pass.

FIGURE 9.10
Circle Captain Volley/Pass.

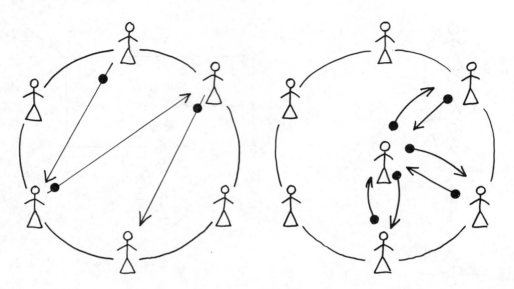

Circle Volley/Pass (Figure 9.9)

1. Arrange six to eight players in a circle six to eight feet in diameter.
2. The player with the ball volleys or passes to a player across the circle.
3. Players continue to volley or pass the ball to different players across the circle, avoiding the players to either immediate side.

Variation

When many balls are available, form groups of three students in triangles. Each student passes or volleys to each person in turn in the triangle.

Circle Captain Volley/Pass (Figure 9.10)

1. Six players form a circle. The seventh player stands in the middle of the circle with a ball.
2. The player in the middle volleys or passes the ball to any player in the circle.
3. The player receiving the ball volleys or passes it back to the middle player.
4. This procedure continues until each player volleys the ball to the center player.
5. Rotate the center player.

FIGURE   9.11
Shifting Center Volley/Pass.

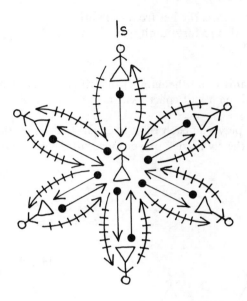

Variation

When volleying the ball back and forth, the player in the middle must volley to each player in turn, moving clockwise.

Shifting Center Volley/Pass (Figure 9.11)

1. Six to eight players stand in a circle. One other player stands in the middle of the circle.
2. One of the perimeter players volleys or passes the ball to the center player, who sends the ball to the next perimeter player (moving clockwise). As the center player plays the ball, the first perimeter player moves to the center position. The center player moves to the position vacated on the perimeter.
3. The new center player is now in position to receive the ball from the second perimeter player. As the new center player volleys or passes to the third player on the perimeter, the second player moves to the center position. The center player then moves into the position vacated on the perimeter, so that the two trade places.
4. All players continue to move quickly to play the ball and trade places. The drill continues until all players return to their original positions.

Serve

Partner Serve (Figure 9.12)

1. Position partners across the net from each other.
2. Serve the ball back and forth until players can consistently perform legal serves.

Team Serve (Figure 9.13)

1. Form enough teams to fill the number of half courts available.
2. Each team stands on a half court baseline. One player on each team holds a ball.
3. On a signal, the player in each right back position serves the ball.
4. After the serve, the right back player moves to the opposite left backcourt position.

FIGURE   9.12
Partner Serve.

FIGURE   9.13
Team Serve.

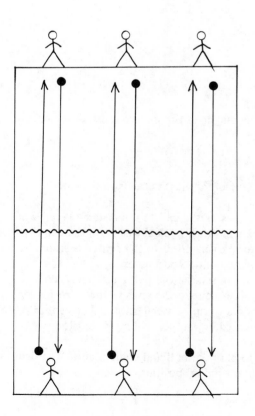

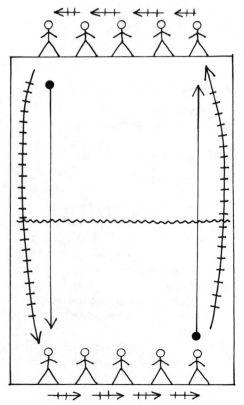

5. All remaining players move one position to the right and a new player serves the ball.
6. Practice continues in this manner until the instructor signals players to stop.

Note: If participants are unable to serve the ball over the net from the right back position, have them move to the center back position or several steps in front of the baseline. Then, after each successful serve, the server moves one step closer to the right back baseline position.

Target Serve (Figure 9.14)

1. Divide each half court into four sections and number them as shown in figure 9.14.
2. Create enough teams to fill the number of half courts available. Each team stands on the baseline of a half court with a ball.
3. The players in the right back positions serve to a retriever from the opposite team. Before serving, the servers designate one of the numbered areas and the retrievers move to that area. After serving, the server becomes the retriever for the opposite team.
4. The retrievers return the balls to the next servers in the right back position on the *opposite* team. The retrievers then move to the left back position on their team.
5. The new servers designate a numbered square they will serve to, and the former server, now acting as retriever, moves into position.
6. Players on the baseline move one position to the right each time the ball is served.
7. The server receives a point if the served ball lands in the designated area of the court.
8. Play continues until one team accumulates twenty-one points.

Four-Square Serve (Figure 9.15)

1. Divide each half court into four sections and number them as shown in figure 9.15.
2. Create enough teams to fill the number of half courts available. Each team stands on the half court baseline with a ball.
3. The right back player serves to a teammate who retrieves the ball. Before the first player serves, the teacher designates a square on the opposite side of the court and the retriever moves to that square.
4. After serving, the server takes the place of the player in the designated square.
5. The retriever returns the ball to the next server and takes the left back position at the baseline.
6. All players should serve the ball to each of the four squares as designated by the teacher.
7. Practice continues until the teacher signals players to stop.

Set

Diad Set (Figure 9.16)

1. Partners face each other four to six feet apart.
2. One partner tosses the ball softly to the other partner, who sets the ball back to the tosser.
3. The tosser *catches* the ball, then repeats the procedure.
4. After five repetitions, the tosser becomes the setter and play is repeated.

FIGURE   9.14
Target Serve.

FIGURE   9.15
Four-Square Serve.

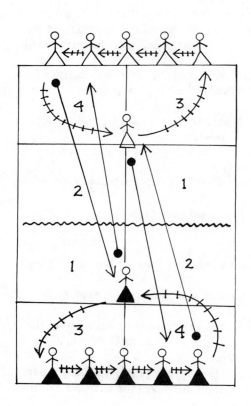

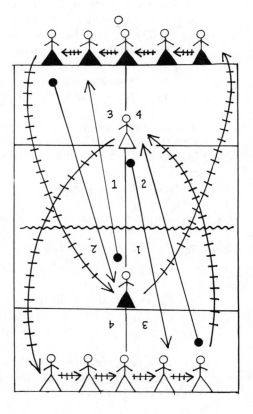

FIGURE   9.16
Diad Set.

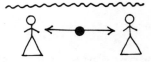

FIGURE   9.17
Triad Set.

FIGURE   9.18
Double-Triad Set.

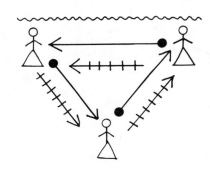

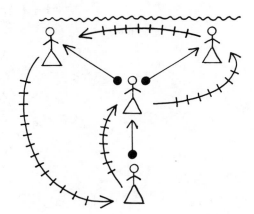

Triad Set (Figure 9.17)

1. A tosser, setter, and catcher form a triad.
2. The tosser tosses to the setter. The setter sets the ball to the catcher. The catcher catches the ball and returns it to the tosser.
3. After repeating this procedure five times, players rotate positions.

Variations

1. The catcher moves around to challenge the accuracy of the setter.
2. When performance merits, the catcher becomes a hitter and hits the ball back to the tosser.

Double-Triad Set (Figure 9.18)

1. One tosser, one setter, and two catchers form a double triad.
2. The tosser tosses the ball to the setter in the center front position (see figure 9.18). The setter sets the ball to either catcher.
3. The catcher who receives the set catches the ball and returns it to the tosser.
4. After the setter has set the ball to each catcher three times, players rotate positions.

FIGURE   9.19
Variation on the Double-Triad Set.

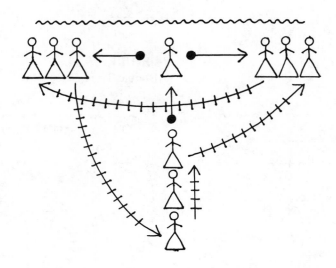

Variations

1. (Figure 9.19) Use a designated setter with six players assigned as catchers and three more assigned as tossers. Rotate catcher and tosser after each toss and set.
2. When performance merits, catchers become hitters and hit the ball back to the next tosser.

Double-Triad-Plus-One Set (Figure 9.20)

1. Four players form a double triad on one side of the court. One player acts as hitter, one as setter, and two are catchers.
2. A fifth player acts as tosser on the opposite side of the net.
3. The tosser tosses the ball over the net to the center back player or hitter (see figure 9.20). This player passes or volleys the ball to the setter in the center front position.
4. The setter sets the ball to either catcher. The catcher catches the ball and returns it to the tosser.
5. All outside players rotate clockwise.

FIGURE   9.20
The Double-Triad-Plus-One Set.

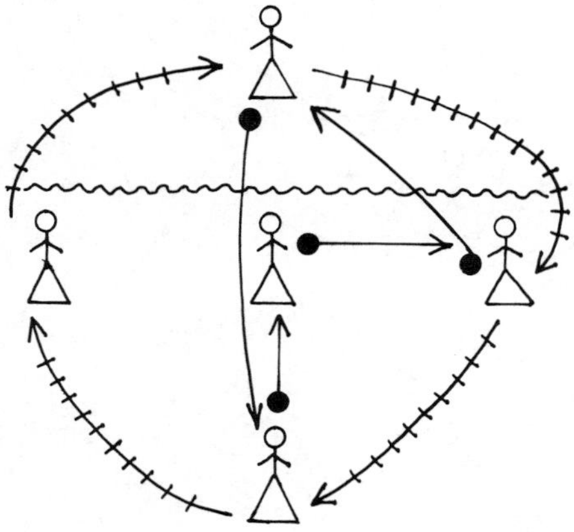

FIGURE   9.21
Set and Hit.

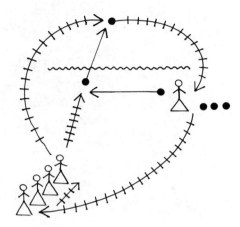

Variations

1. As the players become more skilled, the fifth player serves rather than tosses the ball.
2. The setter rotates upon teacher request. When skill merits, the catchers become hitters.
3. Place two players at each position in the triad instead of one. (This requires eight players plus a ninth player acting as tosser.)

Hit

Set and Hit (Figure 9.21)

1. Four to five hitters form a line at midcourt.
2. A setter stands at midcourt by the net with a ball rack and several balls at hand.
3. The setter, who must be accurate, sets the ball to the first hitter.
4. The hitter moves up to take the set and hits the ball across the net. The hitter then retrieves the ball, returns it to the ball rack beside the setter, and runs to the end of the hitting line.
5. The setter repeats the process with the next hitter. The setter rotates upon teacher request.

FIGURE   9.22
Triad Set and Hit.

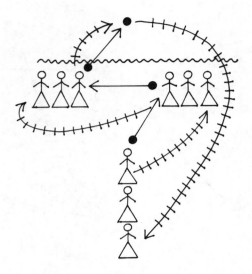

Triad Set and Hit (Figure 9.22)

1. Several tossers, setters, and hitters form a triad.
2. The first tosser tosses to the first setter, who sets the ball to the first hitter. The hitter hits the ball over the net, then retrieves the ball and moves to the end of the tosser line.
3. After the pattern, players rotate one position so that the tosser becomes the setter, the setter becomes the hitter, and the hitter becomes the tosser.

Double-Triad Set and Hit (Figure 9.23)

1. A tosser, a setter, and several hitters form one double triad on each side of the net.
2. The tosser stands at midcourt and tosses the ball to the setter at center front (see figure 9.23). The setter sets the ball to either hitter.
3. The hitter hits the ball over the net, retrieves the ball, and returns to the end of hitting line, giving the ball to the tosser.
4. After each hitter has hit the ball twice, hitters change positions with the tosser and setter.
5. Players rotate until every player has had adequate practice in all positions.

Variation

The setter may be permanent and not rotate.

FIGURE   9.23
Double-Triad Set and Hit.

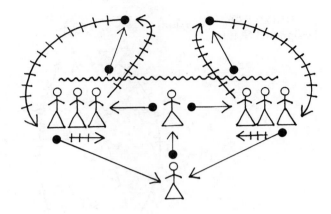

FIGURE   9.24
Double-Triad-Plus-One Set and Hit.

FIGURE   9.25
Variation on the Double-Triad-Plus-One Set and Hit.

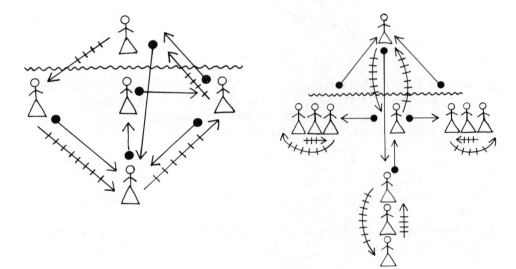

Double-Triad-Plus-One Set and Hit (Figures 9.24 and 9.25)

1. Four players form a double triad.
2. A fifth player acts as tosser on the opposite side of the net.
3. The tosser tosses the ball over the net to the center back player (see figure 9.24). This player passes or volleys the ball to the setter in the center front position.
4. The setter sets the ball to either hitter.

FIGURE   9.26
Designated Setter.

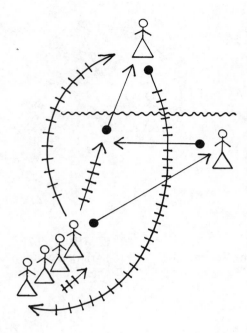

5. After each hit, players rotate as follows: the left hitter becomes the passer, the passer becomes the right hitter, the right hitter becomes the tosser, and the tosser becomes the left hitter. After the fourth hit, the setter exchanges positions with one of the hitters. (However, the player who sets must be skilled enough to set accurately.)

Variations

1. As players become more skilled, the fifth player may serve rather than toss the ball.
2. Add more players to the passer and hitter lines. Players then rotate as shown in figure 9.25.

Designated Setter (Figure 9.26)

Note: This drill is used after setters have been identified so that hitters practice with assigned setters.

1. Position four hitters at side-court, one setter at the net at midcourt, and one retriever across the net.
2. Each hitter has a ball. The hitter tosses the ball to the setter, who sets it back to the hitter. The hitter then hits to the retriever and moves to take over the retriever position.
3. The retriever receives the ball and takes it to the end of the hitting line.

Dig

Partner Dig (Figure 9.27)

1. Partners face each other ten to twelve feet apart.
2. The tosser tosses the ball to the right of the digger. The digger digs the ball back to the tosser.
3. The tosser alternates sending the ball to the right and left sides of the receiver.
4. After a specified number of tosses and digs, players exchange positions.

Horizontal Line Dig (Figure 9.28)

1. A tosser faces a horizontal line of players standing four to five feet apart. Retrievers stand behind the tosser.
2. The tosser, with at least four available balls, tosses a ball to the right or left of the first player. This player digs the ball. The tosser continuously tosses balls to each player in the horizontal line.
3. The retrievers field each ball and keep the tosser supplied with balls.
4. After each player in the horizontal line has had several turns to dig the ball, all players rotate.

File Line Dig (Figure 9.29)

1. Four players form a file line. A tosser stands six to ten feet in front of the file line with two to four balls at hand. A retriever stands behind the tosser.

FIGURE   9.27
Partner Dig.

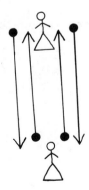

FIGURE   9.28
Horizontal Line Dig.

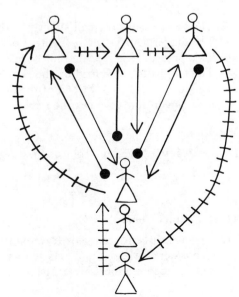

FIGURE   9.29
File Line Dig.

FIGURE   9.30
Three-Contact Court Play.

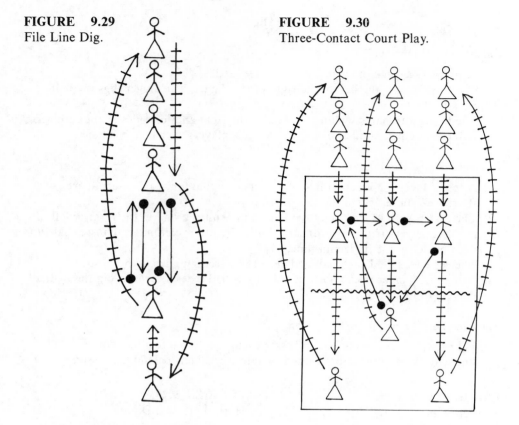

2. The tosser tosses the ball slightly to the right of the first person in the dig line.
3. The digger returns the ball with a one-hand dig.
4. This procedure is repeated to the left.
5. The two balls are fielded by the retriever, who then becomes the tosser.
6. The tosser moves to the end of the dig line.
7. The digger now becomes the retriever.

Variation

Players practice dives and rolls as they dig.

Court Play

Three-Contact Court Play (Figure 9.30)

1. Arrange three players as a team on the court to receive the ball. Another player stands across the net and acts as tosser. Two retrievers position themselves behind and on either side of the tosser.

FIGURE   9.31
Baseline Serve and Play.

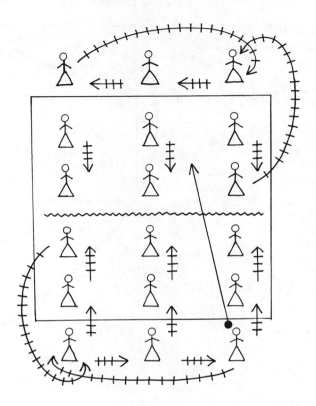

2. The remainder of the players, grouped in teams of three, stand ready to rotate into court positions.
3. The tosser tosses the ball across the net to the three players on the court, who act as a team. Each of the three players must play the ball before sending it back over the net. Possible combinations the threesome can use to return the ball include but are not limited to the following:
   a. Bump, bump, bump
   b. Bump, volley, volley
   c. Volley, set, volley
   d. Bump, set, hit
4. The retrievers and the tosser remain in position until each threesome has had a turn. Then they rotate to the end of the line and the first threesome moves across the net to toss and retrieve.

Baseline Serve and Play (Figure 9.31)

1. Six receivers take positions on each side of the court. The remaining players act as servers and stand behind the baseline on each side of the court.
2. The ball is put into play by a server. The receivers on the court play the ball under regulation rules and keep score. The server does not enter into the court play.

FIGURE   9.32
Five-Serve Court Play.

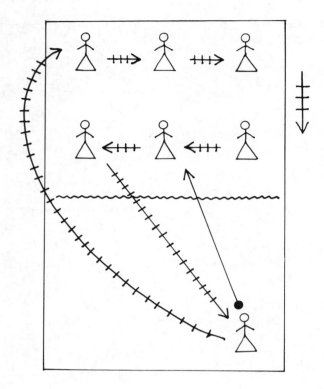

3. Each time one team makes a point, the servers rotate one position to serve the ball. Players on the court do not rotate.
4. After each server has served, these players move forward to court positions. The receivers become the new servers.
5. Every time players rotate onto the court, each player must find a new position (one that particular player has not yet occupied).

Five-Serve Court Play (Figure 9.32)

1. Position a regulation team on one side of the court.
2. Assign one player to the serving position on the opposite side of the court to execute five serves.
3. After each serve, the receiving team must contact the ball three times. The third player must send the ball over the net.
4. After the third contact, play terminates. The server retrieves the ball and serves again. (Assigning an extra person to retrieve out-of-bounds balls helps to increase the speed of the drill.)
5. After five serves, the server rotates to the right back position on the opposite court.

FIGURE   9.33
Team Serve.

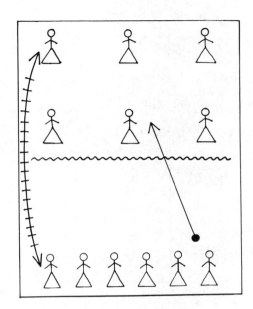

6. The remaining back row players move one position to the left. The left back player moves forward to a front row position.
7. The front row players move one position to the right. The right front player now moves under the net to take the vacated server's position.

Variation

The receiving team practices playing a hard-hit ball. The server becomes a hitter and either stands on a stable box, table, or referee stand close to the net to toss the ball downward or hits a self-tossed ball to the receiving team.

Team Serve (Figure 9.33)

1. Position a serving team on one side of the court and a receiving team on the other.
2. The right back player on the serving team serves the ball. The receiving team must play the ball by making *three* legal contacts.
3. Each player on the serving team serves two balls. After each server has completed both serves, all players move one position using official rotation procedures.
4. After twelve serves, the serving team becomes the receiving team and the receiving team serves.
5. The serving team scores a point each time the receiving team fails to return the ball. The receiving team earns a point each time the serve is illegal.

FIGURE   9.34
Twelve-Plus-One Court Play.

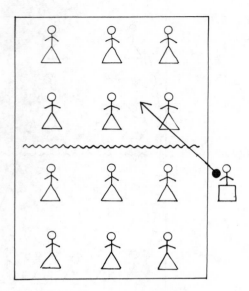

Twelve-Plus-One Court Play (Figure 9.34)

1. Two teams assume court positions. A thirteenth person is designated as tosser/ server.
2. The tosser/server may stand any place on or outside the server's court to toss the ball to any player on the team across the net.
3. After tossing or serving the ball, the tosser/server moves quickly off the court and does not enter into play.
4. The tosser/server continues to put the ball in play from the server's side until side-out. The tosser/server then moves to the other side of the court and becomes the tosser/server for the serving team.
5. Score points as for a regulation game.

LEAD-UP GAMES

Many drills and court-play situations can be developed into lead-up games. Award points for well-executed drills and then determine when players are ready to use their skills in a regulation game.

Cage Ball Volleyball (Grades 4–12)

This game is suitable for all grade levels. The size of the ball, the number of players on a team, and the number of hits per side may vary for different grade levels.

Equipment

Cage ball, net, poles, standards

Procedures

1. Position two teams, with any number of players, on the court.
2. The right back player on the serving team tosses the ball into play. The other players on the serving team may perform up to two assists to get the ball over the net.
3. Each team may hit the ball as many times as needed to return it over the net.
4. When the ball, hits the floor, goes out of bounds without being touched, or is caught or held rather than hit, the teacher calls "point" or "side out."
5. Players rotate according to a standardized system based on the number of players per team. For example:

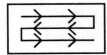 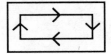

6. Tally the score as for a regulation volleyball game.

Serve Ball (Grades 4–12)

This game is intended to assess each player's serve and provide additional serving practice.

Equipment

Volleyball, net, standards

Procedures

1. Position two teams on the court.
2. The right back player on one team serves the ball, and the defensive team catches any legal serve. Each legal serve counts one point for the team serving. The server continues to serve as long as the serve is legal.
3. Each time the server serves illegally, the other team wins the serve.
4. The first team to score fifteen points and be ahead by two is the winner.

Skill Ball

This game is played to improve specific skills.

Equipment

Volleyball, net, standards

Procedures

1. Position two teams on the court.
2. Designate a specific type of hit, or combination of skills, that players must use after the serve.
3. Enforce all other rules governing a regulation volleyball game.

Ideal Play

This game teaches winning strategy and teamwork.

Equipment

Volleyball, net, standards

Procedures

1. Position two teams on the court.
2. Players must contact the ball three times on each side of the net. Teams are to execute a pass (usually a forearm pass), then a set, and finally a hit. This sequence is the "ideal play."
3. Enforce all other rules governing a regulation volleyball game.

Variation

When one team performs an "ideal play" in a regular game, award two points.

Three on Three

This game emphasizes teamwork and court movement.

Equipment

Volleyball, net, standards

Procedures

1. Position two teams of three players each on each half court.
2. Play official volleyball rules.

SKILL TESTS

Consecutive Volleys/Passes

Mark a line on the wall at least as high as the net. (The suggested net height is eight feet for the forearm pass, eleven feet for the volley.) Toss or volley the ball to get it started. After the initial toss, count the number of consecutive, *legal* volleys or passes performed against the wall on or above the line. Carefully monitor for legal volley/pass executions.

Thirty-Second Volley/Pass

Mark a line on the wall at least as high as the net. Toss or volley the ball to get started. After the initial toss, count the number of legal volleys or passes hit on or above the line in thirty seconds.

Volley Checklist

Evaluate each student's volley technique while students volley the ball against a wall or back and forth across a circle. Score from one to five points for execution in the following categories:

TECHNIQUE	POINTS
Fingertip control	
Elbow extension	
Knee extension	
Height of volley	
Control and placement	
Total	

Pass Checklist

Toss the ball so that students must move forward, back, left, and right to volley the ball. As they do so, evaluate volley technique. As an alternative, evaluate students as they volley the ball against a wall or back and forth across a circle. Score from one to five points for execution in the following categories:

TECHNIQUE	POINTS
Arm/elbow position	
Back extension	
Knee extension	
Body position to ball	
Control and placement	
Total	

Serve Execution

Allow each student three warm-up serves. After the warm-up, each student makes ten attempts to serve the ball. Count the number of legal serves that land anywhere in the court. You may also want to require that students perform a specific type of serve.

Serve Placement

Mark the court, designating specific scoring areas. Count the number of points each student earns by placing legal serves in the designated areas. (Again, you may want to require that students perform a specific type of serve.) Allow each student thirteen serves. Add the points for the student's ten best serves to determine each server's score.

	4	
3	1	3
	2	

Set to Target

Position the setter six feet from a basketball hoop. Position another player close to the basket to toss the ball to the setter. The setter must set the ball into the basket. Count the number of baskets made in ten attempts.

Set to Hitter/Catcher

Position the setter at the net in the center of the court. Position two other players as hitters, one on each side of the court. One hitter tosses the ball to the setter and moves to a hitting position. The setter sets the ball back to that hitter. The hitter catches the ball and the action is repeated by the other hitter. Allow each setter ten hits. The score is the number of sets hit accurately enough that the hitters are able to catch them without moving out of position.

Hit

Position an experienced setter at the net. The hitter tosses or sets the ball to the setter. The setter sets the ball for the hitter, who approaches the ball and hits it sharply down into the opposite court. Allow each student ten accurately set hits (don't count hitting attempts if the set is not accurate). Score the number of correctly hit balls out of ten attempts.

WRITTEN TEST

MATCHING

Note: Some answers may be correct for more than one question. Other answers may not be used at all.

a. block	e. volley	i. side out
b. forearm pass	f. hit (spike)	j. receiving team
c. foot fault	g. line violation	k. serve
d. point	h. serving team	l. legal play

_____ 1. The team that puts the ball into play

_____ 2. A ball legally hit three times by the receiving team and then hit out of bounds by the serving team

_____ 3. A ball hit over the net by the serving team and landing on a boundary line

_____ 4. When the server steps on the endline during the act of serving

_____ 5. A defensive play by a front row player

_____ 6. A ball put in play by the right back player

_____ 7. Legally contacting a forcefully hit ball from below the waist

_____ 8. A ball played by the serving team from out of bounds on the third hit

_____ 9. An offensive play by a front row player from above the net into the opposite court

_____ 10. When the serving team makes an error or fails to legally return the ball over the net

_____ 11. When a player on the receiving team touches the net

_____ 12. When a player on the receiving team steps on the center line

_____ 13. A ball hit into the net by the serving team and recovered out of the net by the same player

_____ 14. Failure to call the score before serving the ball

_____ 15. A ball that skims the top of the net as it drops into the opponents' court on the serve

TRUE OR FALSE

T   F   16. Six players comprise an official volleyball team.

T   F   17. A team must score at least fifteen points to win a game.

T   F   18. The winning team must be at least three points ahead to win a game.

T   F   19. The server is the left back player on the serving team.

T   F   20. Only the serving team scores points.

T   F   21. The server is allowed only one serve to get the ball over the net.

T   F   22. Balls landing on a line are considered out of bounds.

T   F   23. Reaching over the net is legal.

T   F   24. Only players in the front line may spike the ball.

T   F   25. No player may volley the ball twice in succession.

TEST KEY

1. h	6. k	11. d	16. T	21. T
2. i	7. b	12. 1	17. T	22. F
3. d	8. 1	13. i	18. F	23. F
4. c	9. f	14. 1	19. F	24. T
5. a	10. i	15. i	20. T	25. T

CHAPTER TEN

MULTIAPPLICATION ACTIVITIES

Multiapplication activities can be used in a variety of ways during one or two class periods or for an entire unit of instruction. These multiple-use activities are especially well-suited for rainy days and for special times of the year such as the days preceding school holidays. You may also wish to use these activities for class periods shortened by assemblies—or for "just for fun" days when students take a break from the usual routine.

AEROBIC ROUTINES

Aerobic routines set to music are popular with students and easy to create. Select a popular record or tape with a definite rhythm. Teach skills beginning with simple movements and proceeding to the more complex. Allow ten minutes for warm-up, at least fifteen minutes for vigorous exercise, and ten minutes for cool down. It is helpful to students to outline the routine on a poster or on the chalkboard.

Don't confuse three-to-five-minute exercise routines set to music with aerobic routines. You will find suggestions for creating both types of routines in this chapter under the categories of Coordination Exercises and Skills and Jump Rope (use the skills without the rope).

Sample 4/4 Routine

1. Sixteen counts running in place with arms circling.
2. Sixteen counts Flea Hop (see Coordination Exercises for a description of this movement). Slide hop in the direction of the foot that is raised from the ground, arms moving up and down as for Jumping Jacks.
3. Sixteen counts step kick (moving in a circle), eight to the right and eight to the left, arms moving front and side.
4. Sixteen counts stretching as follows:
   a. Four counts side stretch right (hands on hips, lean right).
   b. Four counts front reach (hands on hips, lean forward).
   c. Four counts stretch left (hands on hips, lean left).
   d. Four counts back stretch (hands on hips, lean back).
5. Sixteen counts pendulum swing (hop on left leg and swing right leg to side; hop on right leg, swing left; arms moving in direction of swing).

6. Sixteen counts Finnish Reel (see Coordination Exercises for a description).
7. Sixteen counts Indian Step Can-Can (see Coordination Exercises).
8. Sixteen counts sprint in place (knees high), moving arms vigorously forward and backward.
9. Repeat 1–8.

ELEMENTARY BALL-HANDLING SKILLS

Rolling Ball Exercises (Grades K–3)

Formation

Group students with partners; begin by forming two lines facing each other.

Equipment

One ball for every two people, cones, hula hoops, bowling pins

Procedures

1. Roll the ball back and forth with a partner.
2. Roll the ball against the wall and catch it when it rebounds.
3. Roll the ball between cones.
4. Roll the ball through a hula hoop.
5. Roll the ball at bowling pins.
6. Roll the ball over your partner.
7. Roll the ball through tunnels made by a partner.
   a. Straddle legs
   b. Spread arms and legs (get down on all fours)

Standing Position Ball Exercises (Grades K–6)

Formation

Students scatter in random formation.

Equipment

One ball per person

Procedures

1. Roll the ball on the floor in a figure-eight formation, using hands to control the ball. Repeat three times, reversing the direction of the ball each time.
2. Roll the ball around the waist.
3. Roll the ball around the neck and shoulders.
4. Create other ways of rolling the ball around the body.

Bouncing Ball Exercises (Grades K–6)

Formation

Students find partners, then pairs scatter around the room.

Equipment

One ball per person

Procedures

1. Bounce the ball to music.
2. Bounce the ball, turn around, and catch it.
3. Bounce the ball while jumping.
4. Bounce the ball against the wall, then catch it as it rebounds.
5. Bounce the ball while running.
6. Bounce the ball with the right hand only.
7. Bounce the ball with the left hand only.
8. Bounce the ball once with the right hand, once with the left hand. Continue bouncing and changing hands.
9. Bounce the ball over a body (Bridges).
10. Bounce the ball to a partner, who catches it.
11. Bounce two balls back and forth to a partner (each partner has a ball).

Throwing Ball Exercises: Underhand, Overhand, Overhead (Grades K–6)

Note: If students are throwing to partners, be sure they know how to catch.

Formation

Students begin in scattered formation, then work in columns, then in a circle.

Equipment

At least one ball for every two people, targets (for example, hula hoop or bowling pins)

Procedures

1. Partners throw and return a ball.
2. An individual
   a. throws the ball against the wall.
   b. throws the ball at a target (for example, a hula hoop or bowling pins) using two hands, then using one hand.
3. In a circle with six to eight students, throw the ball
   a. around the circle.
   b. across the circle.

BEAN BAGS

Bean bags are a versatile piece of equipment and are easy to construct. (See chapter 1 to learn how to construct bean bags). Make or buy enough bean bags to provide each student with a bean bag.

Individual Activities (Grades K–3)

Formation
Students may scatter around the room.

Equipment
One bean bag per student

Procedures
1. Maneuver the bean bag around the waist or between the legs.
2. Toss and catch the bean bag eight times.
3. Toss the bean bag back and forth and from side to side.
4. Toss the bean bag up with one hand and catch it with the other hand.
5. Toss the bean bag from behind and over the opposite shoulder. (Catch it with the opposite hand.)
6. Toss the bean bag to the left or right and move to catch it.
7. Balance the bean bag on one elbow, or on the back of the hand, head, or shoulder while walking in a circle.
8. Run with the bean bag and freeze on command, balancing the bean bag on the body part designated by the teacher.

Group Activities

Formation
Students work with partners, then join a circle.

Equipment
At least one bag for every two students, targets (wastebaskets, barrels, hula hoops)

Procedures
1. Toss the bean bag back and forth to a partner eight times.
2. Hike the bean bag like a football to a partner.
3. Toss the bean bag around a circle of six to eight students as if it were a "hot potato."

Target Activities

1. Toss the bean bag in various ways at stationary targets such as wastebaskets, barrels, hula hoops, or wall targets.
2. Toss the bean bag at moving targets such as a swinging hula hoop or moving person who attempts to catch the bag.

CAGE BALL

A cage ball is an oversized canvas or nylon ball. Choose an appropriate size for the ages and skills of the students.

Push Ball (Grades K–6)

Equipment

One cage ball

Procedures

1. Stand in a circle facing in.
2. Move the cage ball by pushing it back and forth across the circle with hands or feet.

Variations

1. Bounce the ball around or across the circle.
2. Kneel or sit in a circle to bounce or roll the ball.

Line Crab Soccer (Grades 4–12)

Equipment

One cage ball

Procedures

1. Players form two lines facing each other and assume the crab position. (For the crab position, sit with feet flat on the floor, knees bent and hands on the floor behind the body. Lift the buttocks off the floor.) Position the cage ball between the two lines of players.
2. Assign matching numbers to players in each line.
3. Call out one to three numbers. The players assigned those numbers advance toward the ball in crab position, attempting to kick the ball across the opposite line.

4. Line players may defend the line, in crab position, by kicking the ball back to the playing area. Line players may not enter the playing area.
5. Score a point when one team kicks the ball across the opposite team's line.

Variation

Place scooters in the center of the playing area. The players whose numbers are called crab walk to the scooters and sit on them, with their hands still touching the floor behind the scooters. These players then attempt to kick the ball while maneuvering the scooter in the crab position. All other players remain in normal crab position.

Crab Soccer (Grades 4–12)

Equipment

One cage ball, colored vests

Procedures

1. Position players on two teams alternately along imaginary parallel lines throughout the playing area.
2. Players move in the crab position, using only their feet to advance the ball.
3. Score a point when the ball goes over the endline of the opposing team. In a gymnasium, the ball can be played off the wall or any other object, thus eliminating out-of-bounds areas.

Variation

Designate a goal area at both ends of the playing space. Goalies from each team protect their goals, and only goalies are allowed to stand. The rest of the players remain in crab position. Players may only score points when they advance the ball into the hands of the goalie standing in the designated goal area.

Mass Cage Ball (Grades 6–12)

Equipment

One cage ball, nets and standards

Procedures

1. Assign two teams of six to twenty players each to a volleyball court.
2. Play the game like volleyball with the following exceptions:
   a. Server pushes the ball into play using one or both hands. Teammates' help on the serve is limited to three hits.
   b. After the serve, hit the ball as many times as necessary to get it over the net.

Variation

Players sit on the floor. Lower the net to touch the floor and use a small cage ball.

Cage Ball Relays (Grades 3–12)

Equipment

One or two cage balls

Procedures

1. Form shuttle lines or circles.
2. Incorporate various activities and ball sizes, depending on the ages and ability of participants. For example:
   a. Players pass the ball overhead.
   b. Players pass the ball around the circle.
   c. Players leapfrog over the ball.

SKILLS AND COORDINATION EXERCISES

The skills and coordination exercises in this section are designed to motivate students and provide fun, challenging activities. These activities should provide a sense of accomplishment as each student's performance improves.

Simple Skill Activities

Formation

Students may be scattered, in lines, in circles, and so on, according to the instructions for each activity.

Equipment

Mats

Front Lean (Balance) (Figure 10.1)

1. Stand erect, arms at sides and feet together.
2. Center weight on right leg and lean forward, extending left leg back and bending right knee.
3. Place hands in front of right leg, sixteen to eighteen inches apart. (Use a mat for safety.)
4. Lean forward, touch forehead to floor.
5. Push up suddenly with the hands and assume erect starting position without losing balance or using hands to help. Keep left leg extended.

FIGURE 10.1
Front Lean.

FIGURE 10.2
Double Heel Click.

FIGURE 10.3
Dutch Jump.

Double Heel Click (Coordination) (Figure 10.2)

1. Stand erect, hands at sides, feet together.
2. Jump straight up, quickly clicking heels together twice.
3. Return to starting position and repeat three times.

Dutch Jump (Flexibility, Coordination) (Figure 10.3)

1. Stand erect with feet together, hands at sides.
2. Jump high and extend legs, spread to sides and slightly forward.
3. At the same time, lean slightly forward and touch toes with fingertips (legs should be fully extended, without bent knees).

Finger Touch (Flexibility) (Figure 10.4)

1. Stand erect with hands at sides, feet pointed out with heels together.
2. Assume squatting position. Weave the arms between the legs and around the ankles, touching fingertips together in front and keeping the heels on the floor.

Turn Left/Right (Balance, Agility) (Figure 10.5)

1. Stand erect, feet eight to ten inches apart.
2. Jump one-quarter turn to the left, landing with feet together and maintaining balance.
3. Jump one-half turn to the left.
4. Jump three-quarters turn to the left.

FIGURE   10.4
Finger Touch.

FIGURE   10.5
Turn Left/Right.

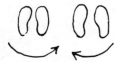

FIGURE   10.6
Tip Up.

FIGURE   10.7
Turk Stand.

5. Make a complete turn to the left, landing with feet together and maintaining balance.
6. Repeat the full turn three times in a row.
7. Repeat the entire sequence to the right.

Tip Up (Strength, Balance) (Figure 10.6)

1. Assume a squatting position on the mat, feet spread apart and pointed out, hands in front of knees and sixteen to eighteen inches apart.
2. Put weight on hands, bend elbows slightly, and lean forward, placing knees on outside of elbows.
3. Lift feet from the floor, shifting weight slightly forward.
4. Maintain balance for five seconds. Tuck head and roll forward if balance is lost.

Turk Stand (Balance, Strength, Flexibility) (Figure 10.7)

1. Cross right leg over left (or left over right) in standing position.
2. Fold arms across chest.
3. Sit down slowly, keeping arms folded and legs crossed.
4. Leaning slightly forward and putting weight on sides of feet, rise to a standing position, keeping the arms folded and the legs crossed.

FIGURE   10.8
Tore Jeté.

FIGURE   10.9
Up Swing.

FIGURE   10.10
Jump Over the Leg.

Tore Jeté (Coordination, Balance) (Figure 10.8)

1. Start on the left foot. Step with the left foot, slide the right foot in next to the left, and step with the left again.
2. As you step with the left foot, kick forward with the right leg and jump, swinging your arms over your head.
3. As you jump, pivot a half turn to left. Land on the right leg with the left leg extended back.

Up Swing (Strength, Balance, Concentration) (Figure 10.9)

1. Assume kneeling position, sitting on heels, hands at sides.
2. Thrust arms back and then swing them forward, jumping to a crouched position on feet.
3. Maintain balance for three seconds and rise to a standing position.

Jump Over the Leg (Concentration, Strength, Agility) (Figure 10.10)

1. Stand on right leg.
2. Lift the left leg, bending the knee, and hold the left toe with the right hand.
3. Attempt to jump over the leg being held by the right hand.
4. Repeat the attempt with the opposite leg.

Coordination Exercises

Formation

Students may be scattered, in lines, in circles, and so on according to instructions for each exercise.

Equipment

None

Jumping Jacks

1. Stand in erect position, hands at sides, feet together.
2. Count 1: Arms move up over head as feet jump out to sides.
3. Count 2: Arms move in against sides as feet jump in together.

Jumping-Jack Variation 1

1. Stand in erect position, hands at sides, feet together.
2. Count 1: Arms move up as feet jump forward.
3. Count 2: Arms move down to beginning position as feet jump back.

Jumping-Jack Variation 2 (Figure 10.11)

1. Stand in erect position, hands at sides, feet together.
2. Count 1: Arms move up over head, feet jump out to sides.
3. Count 2: Arms move back down, feet jump back together.
4. Count 3: Arms move up, feet jump in place together.
5. Count 4: Arms move down, feet jump out to sides.
6. Count 5: Arms move up, feet jump together.
7. Count 6: Arms move down, feet jump in place together.
8. Repeat sequence.

FIGURE   10.11
Jumping Jack Variation 2.

1   2   3   4   5   6

Jumper

1. Stand in erect position, hands at sides, feet together.
2. Feet jump together in place on each count.
3. Count 1: Swing arms forward and over head.
4. Count 2: Swing arms down till shoulder high.
5. Count 3: Swing arms up and over head.
6. Count 4: Swing arms down to starting position at sides.
7. Repeat entire sequence.

Hopper

1. Stand in erect position, hands at sides, feet together.
2. Count 1: Move both arms and right foot forward, touching toe to floor, and hop on left foot.
3. Count 2: Move arms to sides and right foot to right side, and hop on left foot.
4. Count 3: Move arms and right foot back to forward position, and hop on left foot.
5. Count 4: Return to starting position.
6. Reverse to opposite side, repeat sequence, and continue alternating feet every four counts (forward, side, forward, together).

Hopper Syncopation (Figure 10.12)

1. Stand in erect position, hands on shoulders, feet together.
2. Arms alternate movement, returning to shoulder after each count. Legs alternate swinging out in pendulum motion.
3. Count 1: Right arm up; left foot out.
4. Count 2: Left arm up; right foot out.
5. Count 3: Right arm out; left foot out.
6. Count 4: Left arm out; right foot out.
7. Count 5: Right arm forward; left foot out.

FIGURE 10.12

Hopper Syncopation.

1   2   3   4   5   6   7   8

8. Count 6: Left arm forward; right foot out.
9. Count 7: Right arm down; left foot out.
10. Count 8: Left arm down; right foot out.

Flea Hop (Figure 10.13)

1. Stand erect, feet together, hands on hips.
2. Hop to the left on the left foot and place the right foot beside it.
3. Hop to the right on the right foot and place the left foot beside it.
4. Continue moving left and right.

Finnish Reel (Figure 10.14)

1. Stand erect, feet together, hands on hips.
2. Hop on left foot, extending right leg to side and touching toe to floor (sole of foot facing out); hop on left foot again and touch right heel in the same place.
3. Hop on right foot, extending left leg to side and touching toe to floor (sole of foot facing out); hop on right foot again and touch left heel in the same place.
4. Continue moving left and right.

Indian Step (Figure 10.15)

1. Stand erect, feet together, hands on hips.
2. Hop four times on the right foot, touching left toe to floor on counts 1 and 3.
3. Repeat, hopping on the left foot and touching right toe to floor.

Cancan Variation

Kick the free leg forward on count 4.

FIGURE   10.13
The Flea Hop.

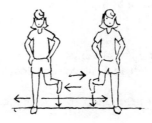

FIGURE   10.14
The Finnish Reel.

FIGURE 10.15
The Indian Step.

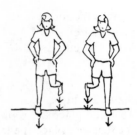

FIGURE 10.16
Bells.

Bells (Figure 10.16)

1. Stand erect, hands on hips, feet slightly apart.
2. Cross left leg over right.
3. Hop on left foot, jump and click heels together, and land on left foot.
4. Cross right leg over left. Hop on right foot, jump and click heels together, and land on right foot.
5. Continue jumping left and right.

Charleston (Figure 10.17)

1. Stand erect, feet together, hands on hips.
2. Count 1: With weight on left foot, place right foot in front of left foot, touching toes to floor.
3. Count 2: Swing right foot behind left foot, stepping onto right foot as it touches the floor.
4. Count 3: Shift weight to right foot and place left foot behind right foot, touching toes to floor.
5. Count 4: Swing left foot in front of right foot, stepping onto left foot as it touches the floor.
6. Repeat the entire sequence (front, behind with right foot; behind, front with left foot).
7. Add two bounces on the supporting foot to each count.

FIGURE   10.17
The Charleston.

FIGURE   10.18
The Pony.

Pony (Figure 10.18)

1. Stand erect, feet together, hands on hips.
2. Count 1: With weight on left foot, place right foot across and in front of left foot.
3. Count 2: Jump to uncrossed position, extending right leg in front and ending with weight on left foot and right heel.
4. Count 3: Jump to crossed position, shifting weight to right foot and extending left foot forward and across in front of right foot.
5. Count 4: Jump to uncrossed position, extending left leg in front and ending with weight on right foot and left heel.
6. Repeat the entire sequence.

JUMP ROPE

Long Rope

Long rope jumping (two students turning and one or more jumping, with no more than eight to a group) is a good lead-up for single rope activities. Students can concentrate on jumping alone without coordinating the turn of the rope with the jump. Build endurance gradually so students can tolerate extended periods of jumping.

Long Rope Activities (Figure 10.19)

1. Continuous Jumps: Progress from five to ten jumps.
2. Two-Person Jump: Two people jump while two others turn the rope.
3. Six-Person Jump: Up to six people jump, coordinating their jumping.
4. Ball Jump: One person jumps while bouncing a ball.
5. Short Rope/Long Rope Jump: One person jumps with a short rope inside a long rope. At the beginning, make sure the long and short ropes turn at the same time. As the student's skill improves, turn the long rope once as the short rope turns twice.
6. Two-Person Short Rope/Long Rope Jump: Two people jump, using a short rope inside a long rope.
7. Cross Ropes: Two ropes cross at right angles to each other. The jumper jumps over both as they come together.
8. Double Dutch: Two parallel ropes turn, alternating as they turn *inward* toward each other. Jumpers jump each turn of each rope.
9. Double French: The same as Double Dutch, but the two parallel ropes alternate as they turn *outward*.

FIGURE 10.19
(a) Continuous Jumps. (b) Two-Person Jump. (c) Six-Person Jump. (d) Ball Jump.
(e) Short Rope/Long Rope Jump. (f) Two-Person Short Rope/Long Rope Jump.
(g) Cross Ropes. (h) Double Dutch. (i) Double French.

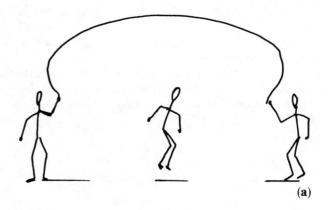

(a)

FIGURE   10.19—*Continued*

FIGURE   10.19—*Continued*

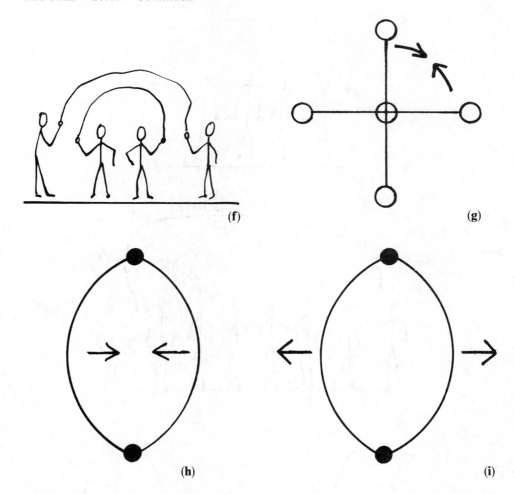

(f)

(g)

(h)

(i)

Short Rope

Each student needs a rope that is the correct length. When the student stands on the rope, the ends should reach to the shoulders.

Continuous daily jumping over extended periods of time may cause injuries. Therefore, interchange other activities with turning and jumping to avoid undue stress.

Short Rope Activities (Figure 10.20)

1. Forward Jump: Jump ten times in place, turning the rope forward.
2. Backward Jump: Jump ten times in place, turning the rope backward.

3. Out-In: Starting with feet together, jump ten times, alternating feet out and in to side stride position (feet apart, together).

4. Cross Legs: Jump, alternating side stride position with a cross-leg position (right over left). Repeat, crossing left over right.

5. Forward-Back: Starting with feet together, jump, alternating feet forward and back in the back stride position (feet apart, one forward, one back).

6. Front Cross: Jump, turning rope forward with uncrossed arms, then with crossed arms. Continue jumping, alternating uncrossed and crossed arms. Repeat five times.

7. Backward Cross: Repeat the front cross, turning the rope backward.

8. Toe Touch: Jump, touching the right toe to the floor behind, then the left toe to the floor behind. Repeat ten times. *Variation:* Jump, touching each toe twice back to the floor before alternating.

9. Step Kick Forward: Jump on both feet, extending one leg forward on every other jump. Repeat ten times, alternating legs.

10. Double Unders: Jump a single jump; then, jump and quickly turn the rope twice before feet touch floor. Repeat.

11. The following routines, described in the Coordination Exercises, can be performed while jumping rope:
    a. Flea Hop
    b. Finnish Reel
    c. Indian Step
    d. Bells
    e. Charleston
    f. Pony

Note: To ensure the safety of the students, perform the following skills in an adequate, unobstructed space.

12. Run Forward: Run forward with one foot each time the rope is turned.

13. Skip Forward: Turn the rope slowly to skip. Move over the rope on each skip (exactly the same as without rope).

14. Polka Forward: Turn the rope slowly to polka. The polka move is hop forward on one foot, step close with the toes of the other foot, step back down on the first foot (hop, step close, step). Repeat, alternating feet. The rope moves under the feet on each step close, step. **Variation:** Rope turns once under the hop and again under the step close, step.

15. Grapevine: Turn the rope forward. Move left, stepping on the left foot, crossing the right foot in front, stepping left, crossing the right foot behind. Repeat four times; then reverse direction, stepping to the right with the right foot. (Turn the rope on each step.) The transition to the right should be smooth, with the rope continuing to turn without stopping.

FIGURE   10.20
(a) Forward Jump. (b) Backward Jump. (c) Out-In Jumping. (d) Cross-Leg
Jumping. (e) Forward-Back. (f) Front Cross. (g) Backward Cross. (h) Toe Touch.
(i) Step Kick Forward. (j) Double Unders.

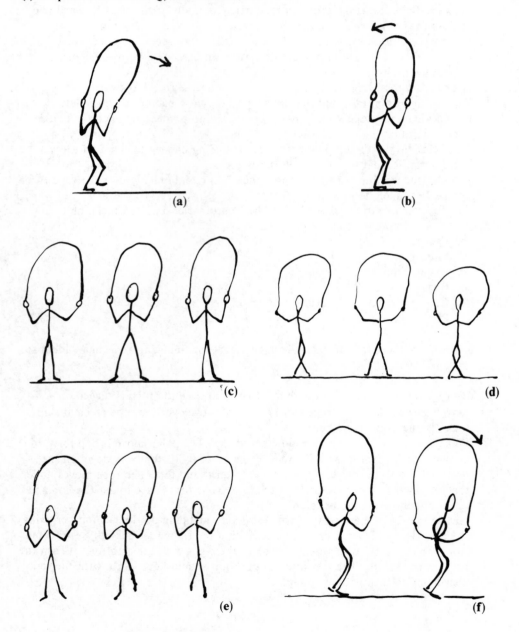

FIGURE   10.20—*Continued*

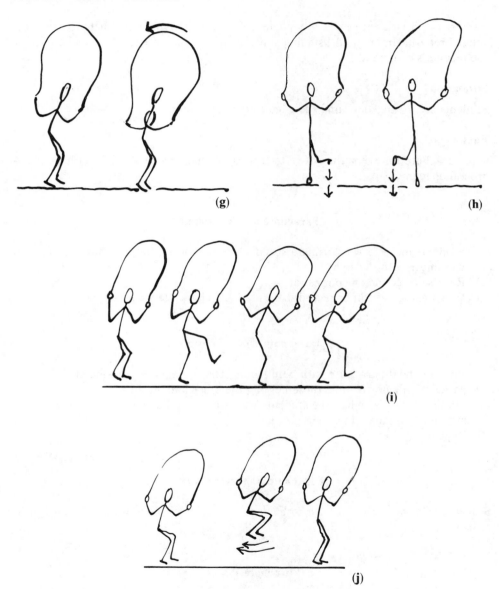

(g)

(h)

(i)

(j)

PARACHUTES

Parachute activities are especially popular with younger students. Such activities develop strength, timing, and listening skills. Students should execute each activity on the teacher's command.

Formation

Students are arranged around the edge of the parachute.

Equipment

One parachute for every thirty-five to forty students, fleeceballs or bean bags, playground or tennis balls

Parachute Circle Around

1. Students move forward using a specified locomotor movement while holding the parachute with the right hand.
2. Reverse direction on command.
3. When using a drum or record, have students clap cadence first.

Parachute Up and Down

1. Students hold parachute with both hands. The students on one side of the parachute lie down while those holding the other half sit up.
2. On the teacher's signal, the students who are sitting lie down, pulling the remaining students to sitting position.
3. Repeat.

Parachute Shake-the-Rug

Students hold the parachute with both hands at waist level and move it with rapid little shakes.

Parachute Waves

Students hold the parachute with both hands and move it up above the head and down with big muscle movements.

Parachute Mushroom

1. Students kneel around the parachute.
2. On command, students lift parachute above their heads.
3. On the teacher's command, they move arms rapidly to the ground, allowing air to make the parachute look like a mushroom.

Variation

After making the mushroom, students move from kneeling to sitting, bringing parachute rapidly overhead and down to the ground so all students are sitting inside the chute.

Parachute Dome

1. Students stand around the parachute.
2. Place the parachute on the floor and pull tight.
3. On the teacher's command, students lift the chute high overhead to form a dome.

Variations

1. As students raise the parachute to form the dome, they take small, slow steps in. As the parachute drops, they move in small, slow steps back to their original positions.
2. While the dome is in the air, groups of students change places on the teacher's command by walking, hopping, or skipping while the rest hold on. Possible groups include:
   a. Every other student around the circle
   b. All the boys or all the girls
   c. Everyone wearing a certain color
   d. Everyone with a birthday in a certain month
   e. Everyone with a certain eye or hair color

Parachute Ball

Students hold the parachute with both hands at waist level and move a ball around the edge of the chute, trying to keep the ball from falling off.

Parachute Popcorn

1. Students hold the parachute at waist level.
2. Using such objects as bean bags or fleeceballs, students shake the parachute, tossing the objects into the air like popping popcorn.

Parachute Hole-in-One

1. Students hold the parachute at waist level.
2. Using a bean bag or ball set onto the chute, the students attempt to shake the object into the hole in the middle of the parachute.

Variation

Assign teams and give each team several pompoms, using one color per team. Arrange the pompoms on the parachute in front of each team and score a point for a team each time they shake one of their pompoms through the hole.

RELAYS

Relays help build comraderie and team spirit. They are not effective for skill practice when achievement is determined by speed rather than quality of performance.

Formation

Students may position themselves in file or shuttle lines.

Equipment

Cones or line markers, batons, balls, bean bags, blocks, cage ball, jump ropes, wands, hoops

Locomotor Skills Relays

Students perform such movements as running, skipping, hopping, galloping, or jumping in relay teams.

Baton Relays

1. Pass the baton over the shoulders.
2. Pass the baton between the legs.
3. Pass the baton back and forth in shuttle formation.

Ball Relays

1. Dribble the ball.
2. Dribble the ball around an obstacle, for example, cones.
3. Pass the ball over the shoulders and between the legs while running.
4. Roll the ball between the legs while running.

5. Throw the ball into the air and catch it (juggle) while running, hopping, skipping, or jumping.
6. Dribble the ball on the way down, juggle it on the way back.
7. Dribble the ball down to a wall, pass it against the wall, dribble it back.

Bean Bag Relays

1. Run and juggle the bean bags (toss it and catch it as you run).
2. Hop with a bean bag between the knees or ankles.
3. Balance a bean bag on various body parts (such as head, elbow, arm, or shoulder) while walking, running, hopping, or skipping.
4. Throw the bean bag to the first person in the opposite shuttle line and go to end of that line.

Block Relays (Grades K–3)

Note: Each member of the relay team needs one block.

1. Each member of the team adds a block to a stack.
2. Arrange the blocks in a line.
3. Place a block of a certain color or shape on the top or bottom of the stack.
4. Balance the block on one part of the body such as head, elbow, arm, shoulder, or lower back.

Cage Ball Relays

Use activities described in the Cage Ball section of this chapter and adapt them for relay teams.

Jump Rope Relays

Note: Each relay team needs one rope.

1. Skip in a forward direction while jumping rope.
2. Run forward while jumping rope.
3. Refer to the Jump Rope section in this chapter for more ideas.

Wand Relays

1. Two students hold a wand as each team member jumps over it.
2. Balance the wand and run, skip, or hop.
3. Move objects such as a hula hoop, ball, or block with the wand.
4. Balance the wand on various body parts such as head, elbow, arm, or shoulder.
5. Push the wand using various body parts.

Hoop Relays

1. Run or walk while spinning the hoop on various body parts such as arm, neck, waist.
2. Progress forward, turning the hoop like a jump rope and jumping through it.
3. Hop, jump, or leap through an obstacle course composed of hoops.
4. Roll the hoop while moving forward.
5. Throw the hoop in the air three to five times and catch it while moving.

SCOOTERS

Scooters provide the student and teacher with a wonderful change of pace. If used over a long period of time they can help students develop strength, balance, and coordination. However, scooters can contribute to accidents and injuries. Students should not be permitted to stand on scooters or engage in reckless behavior.

Formation

Students line up as for a relay (in file lines), with four to six students to a line.

Equipment

Two scooters per line (minimum)

Scooter Scoot

Student sits on scooter, using feet to roll forward to a designated spot and back to the starting line using hands to grasp or balance the scooter.

Kneel Scoot

Students kneel on the scooter and use their arms to propel the scooter forward and back to the starting line.

One-Foot Scoot

Students kneel on the scooter with one knee, holding the sides of the scooter with their hands. They then use the other foot to propel the scooter forward. Students change position at the halfway mark, using the opposite foot to propel the scooter back to the starting line.

Swim Scoot

Students place their stomachs and thighs on the scooters, keeping their legs and feet off the floor. They then use only their arms to propel the scooters to a designated line or mark.

You-and-Me Scoot

Students kneel or sit on the scooters. If they sit, they should cross their legs in front, keeping their backs straight and stiff. In either case, students must *hold on to the sides of the scooter and keep a straight, stiff back to avoid being pushed off the scooter.* A partner pushes the person to the designated line or mark and back again.

Triple Scoot

Students sit or kneel as just described. One person on either side of the scooter holds the riders hands and pulls the scooter to the designated line or mark. A new rider (one of the pullers) then sits or kneels on the scooter and is pulled back to the start.

Wheelbarrow Scoot

Students place their chests on the scooters, holding onto the sides of the scooters with both hands and extending the legs straight back. The partner picks up the rider's legs (do not bend the knees) from behind and pushes the scooter forward to a designated line. Partners may change places to return to the starting line. *Never use this relay with a wall as a finish line.*

TAG GAMES

Students of all ages enjoy tag activities. One can easily create enough tag game variations to consume a regular class period. Move from one game to another smoothly and quickly.

Touch Tag

Designate one player as "IT." When IT tags another player, that player becomes IT. Give each player a ball or a hula hoop and require players, including IT, to dribble the ball or roll the hoop as they move around.

Locomotor Tag

Play this game like Touch Tag, but require players to skip, hop, jump, or slide to move around.

Hold Tag

This game requires players to assume a certain position to be safe from IT. For example, to avoid being tagged, each player might have to kneel down on one knee, wind an arm under the leg that is not kneeling, and hold the nose.

Freeze Tag (Grades K–3)

Designate one person as IT for the entire game. As players are tagged they must immediately freeze in whatever position and place they are in. The game continues until everyone is "frozen." The last person tagged becomes IT for the next game.

Cap Tag

IT carries a cap and hands the cap to the player tagged. Players continue to pass the cap around in this manner. At the end of a short time period, the person who ends up with the cap is designated IT.

Elbow Tag

Partners stand with elbows hooked, their outside (loose) hands on their hips. Designate one person as IT and select one or two other individuals to be chased (two if an odd number of players exist). The chased player(s) must hook onto one of the outside arms of any set of partners before being tagged. When the hook-up occurs, the partner of the person hooked must run and hook another arm before being tagged by IT. Anyone tagged before hooking arms becomes IT.

Exchange Tag

Two lines of players face each other on opposite sides of a playing area. IT stands in the middle of the playing area. The teacher calls two to four names (or numbers) from each line and these persons exchange places, trying to avoid being tagged by IT. Any player tagged becomes IT.

Variation

IT calls the name of a player, and then that player calls a name on the opposite team. The two players attempt to exchange places before IT tags either person.

Spot Ball Tag (Grades K–3)

Two people, usually a boy and a girl, are designated as IT. Each has a ball. Each IT places the ball behind someone of the opposite sex, who picks up the ball and chases that IT around the circle, attempting to tag IT. If the runners tag each IT, the runners can return to their places. Any runner who is unsuccessful in tagging one of the ITs becomes a new IT.

Spoke Tag

Divide the group into even lines with three or four players to a line. Form the lines so that each represents a spoke in a large wheel, with each line seated facing the center of the wheel. One person, acting as IT, jogs around the outside of the wheel. IT selects a spoke, stops, and tags the last person of that spoke on the back. The last person rises, tagging the person just ahead. That person then rises and tags the next member of the spoke. This continues until each person in the spoke has been tagged. After everyone in the line has risen, the individual members of the spoke and IT may race around the outside of the circle, trying to avoid being last. No one can move out of line until the person nearest the center of the spoke starts to run; then all must race in the same direction. The last one to get around and be seated in the spoke line becomes IT.

WANDS

Wands may be used to develop hand-eye coordination, flexibility, and strength. Provide a wand for each student and allow adequate space for all activities. (Wands may be round or flat, but should be approximately one-by-one-inch pieces of wood from thirty to thirty-six inches in length.)

Individual Wand Challenge Activities

1. Balance the wand on various body parts: head, elbow, shoulder, and finger.
2. Move over, around, and under the wand.
3. Balance the wand on the floor. Release the wand; then try to complete a stunt and catch the wand before it hits the floor. For example, turn around three times, clap hands five times, or click heels before catching the wand.
4. Pick up the wand with your toes.
5. Hold the wand in front of your body at or below waist level, grasping each end with one hand. Jump over the wand and back without losing your grip on either end.

Wand Exercises

1. **Flexibility Climb**: Grip the wand at each end and hold it in front of the body. Without losing your grip on either end, step over the stick with the right leg. Bring the left arm over the head and slide the stick around the body; then, slide the wand under the hip and step through with the left leg. When you finish, your palms will be facing outward. Now reverse the procedure and climb over the wand backwards. Return to starting position, moving backward through the wand.
2. **Walk Wand** (for strengthening fingers): Hold the wand vertically in front of the body. Starting with one hand at the bottom end, use the fingers to "walk up" and then down the wand. Try with one hand, then the other hand.
3. **Twister** (for strengthening wrists and arms): Grasp the wand in the middle with both hands. Hold it in front of the body and rotate it forward with the right hand and backwards with the left hand.

RECREATIONAL GAMES

These games were selected because of their continued popularity with students of all ages.

Crows and Cranes (Grades K–4)

Equipment

None

Procedures

1. Divide the class into two teams: the Crows and the Cranes.
2. Mark two goals approximately fifty feet apart. Position teams so that they face each other in between both goals, about five feet apart.

3. The teacher calls out either "Crows" or "Cranes," emphasizing the cr-r-r-r sound. The team that the teacher finally calls then chases the other team to their goal. Anyone caught in the middle becomes a member of the other team.
4. At the end of the playing time, the team with the most players is the winner.

Variations

1. Teams face away from each other to start the game.
2. The leader tells a story using as many words beginning with "cr" as possible (for example, crazy, crunch, critter, crowd, crude, crown). The teacher should emphasize the cr-r- r-r-r sound each time. No one may move on any of the words except "crows" or "cranes."

Four Square (Grades K–6)

Equipment

Ball (playground or volleyball)

Procedures

1. Mark an area ten feet square and divide this area into four equal parts. Designate the squares as 1, 2, 3, and 4. Mark a diagonal service line in the box designated as number 1.
2. Assign one player to stand in each of the designated areas.
3. The player behind the diagonal line in square 1 serves underhand, on the bounce, to any other box. Any serve that hits a line is out.
4. The receiver directs the ball to any other square with an underhand hit.
5. The following are faults:
   a. An illegally served ball
   b. Hitting the ball sidearm or overhand
   c. Causing the ball to land on a line between squares rather than on an outer boundary
   d. Stepping into another square to play the ball
   e. Catching or carrying a return
   f. Allowing the ball to touch any part of the body other than the hands
   g. Failing to return the ball
6. When a player commits a fault, play stops and that player immediately moves to the number 4 square. All other players move up one square. (If anyone other than the server faults, the server remains in square 1 and all other players move up one square.)
7. Extra players may rotate into the game when a fault is committed.
8. The person in square 1 at the end of the playing period is declared the winner.

Steal the Bacon (Grades K–12)

Equipment

Bean bag, knotted towel, or other suitable article

Procedures

1. Outline a three-to-five foot circle halfway between two goal lines thirty to fifty feet apart.
2. Divide the class into two teams and position one team on each goal line. Assign identical numbers to players on each team.
3. Place a bean bag (or other article) in the center of the circle to represent the "bacon" and designate a guard to protect the "bacon."
4. The teacher calls out a number. The players with this number (one from each team) must attempt to steal the bacon and cross their team's goal line before being tagged by the guard.
5. If a player is tagged, that player changes places with the guard. Any player who gets the bacon across the goal line scores a point.

Variations

1. Call two or more numbers from each team.
2. Place the bacon in the circle without a guard. Players race for the bacon and try to get it back behind their goal line without being tagged. They may drop the bacon or toss it to a teammate to avoid being tagged by an opposing player. If a player drops the bacon, the attempt to steal it is repeated.

Ten Pass (Grades K–12)

Equipment

Home plate, one base, one ball (eight-and-a-half inches in diameter)

Procedures

1. Play this game in a gymnasium or on an outside playing field.
2. Position a home base. Place another base (or other marker) along the outside playing boundary thirty to sixty feet from home base. The players' skill determines the distance between home plate and the marker.
3. Divide the class into two teams: one team in the playing area and the other behind home base in kicking order.
4. On the fielding team, a pitcher stands approximately thirty feet from home base and rolls the ball to the kicker. Each kicker receives no more than three pitched balls.
5. The kicker must kick the ball, run to the marker, and run back to home base. Any player who kicks a foul ball is out.

6. The fielding team tries to make an out in one of two ways: by catching the kicked ball on the fly, or by completing ten passes before the kicker returns to home base.
7. Players on the fielding team may not stand closer than five feet away from one another when passing. A player may not catch the ball more than once until all players have passed the ball. After receiving a pass, each player should kneel or sit down to avoid receiving the ball again.
8. If a fielding player fails to catch the ball, the fielding team must continue to throw until ten good catches are made.
9. After the kicking team makes three outs, the teams change places.

Variation

Use different kinds of balls. For example, punt a football to begin play and then pass the ball.

Safety Zone Ball (Grades 6–12) (Figure 10.21)

Equipment

Playground ball

Procedures

1. Play this game in the gymnasium.
2. Designate a ten-foot safety zone at one end of the playing area and a five-foot restraining area at the opposite end. Place a home plate in the middle of the restraining area (see figure 10.21).
3. Divide the class into two teams.
4. Position the defensive team anywhere between the safety zone and the restraining line. Designate one player as the pitcher, and position this player at the foul line.
5. The offensive team arranges themselves in a hitting order and the first player takes position at home plate. The remaining players line up behind home plate and inside the restraining area.
6. The pitcher bounces the ball to the hitting player at home plate.
7. The hitting player strikes the ball with an arm or fist before running to the safety zone.
8. The player running to the safety zone may remain there through the turn of one additional player, but then must return across the restraining line.
9. The hitting team scores one run for each player who runs to the safety zone and back without making an out.
10. The fielding team can make an out in one of two ways: by catching the offensive player's hit on the fly, or by throwing the ball and hitting the offensive player below the waist with it.
11. The hitting team is allowed three outs. Then the two teams exchange positions.

Hit-Pin Kickball (Grades 4–12) (Figure 10.22)

Equipment

Four bowling pins, one ball (eight-and-a-half inches in diameter)

Procedures

1. Play this game in a gymnasium. Create a diamond by placing four bowling pins equal distances apart, with the home-base pin on one end line between the foul lines.
2. Divide the class into two teams, one offensive and one defensive.
3. The defensive team has a pitcher, a catcher, three basemen, and any number of fielders. The basemen must stand inside the pin to create an out or to reset the pin.
4. The offensive team designates a kicking order.

FIGURE   10.21
Safety Zone Ball Court.

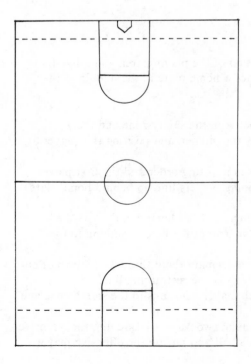

FIGURE   10.22
Hit-Pin Kickball "Diamond."

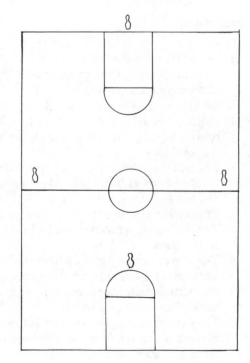

5. The pitcher rolls the ball to the first player. Each kicker receives no more than three pitched balls.
6. The player kicks the ball and runs the diamond, passing outside the pins until reaching "home plate." The runner may not stop running until reaching home plate.
7. The kicking team scores one run each time a kicker crosses home plate without making an out.
8. Any kicker is out (a) when a foul ball is kicked, (b) after failing to kick any of the three pitched balls, or (c) after knocking down any of the pins while running.
9. The kicker is also out when the fielding team
    a. catches the kick on the fly.
    b. knocks down the first-base pin with the ball before the kicker passes the pin. (If the kicker is not out at the first-base pin, the kicker continues to run past all the pins in order and may only be put out at the home-base pin.)
    c. knocks down each pin in order before the kicker runs past the home-base pin.
10. The two teams exchange positions after the kicking team makes three outs.

Variations

1. Play the game outside on a softball diamond. Substitute cones for pins, and instruct the players to touch each cone without knocking it down as they run by.
2. Send two players to home plate at the same time, with one designated to kick the ball. One player runs to first, second, third, and home and the other player runs the reverse—to third, second, first, and then home. The fielding team may attempt to knock the pins down by throwing in either sequence, depending on where the ball was originally fielded. If one player is out at either first or third, the other player may continue to run. The fielding team must attempt to get that player out at home by knocking down the pins in the order the player is running. In this variation, it is possible to score two runs after each kick.

Swedish Grounders (Grades 6–12)

Equipment

Three bases, one playground ball

Procedures

1. Position two teams on a softball diamond with one team in the field and the other up to bat.
2. The fielding team designates a pitcher, a catcher, and first, second, and third basemen. Other players may take any position on the field.
3. The pitcher must stand on the designated pitching spot and *bounce* the ball to the batter to hit.

4. The batter hits the ball with the arm. Each batter is allowed two strikes.
5. When the ball is hit, the batter runs to first base and then to second and third.
6. The batting team scores a run each time a batter crosses home plate before the last out.
7. A runner is not required to run if it is probable that an out will be made. Any number of runners may be on any base at any time. After leaving the base, the runner must go back to that base or reach the next before the fielding team touches the base with the ball.
8. The batter is out when
   a. the batter makes three strikes.
   b. the fielding team catches a hit on the fly.
   c. the fielding team throws the ball to the pitcher or to any baseman, who then touches the ball to the pitching mark or base before the runner reaches a base.
9. The batting team is allowed four outs. Should all players be caught on base with no one to bat, the entire team is retired and the fielding team is up to bat.

Volley Tennis (Grades 6–12)

Volley tennis is a combination of volleyball and tennis. This lively, easy-to-learn activity integrates some of the rules, skills, and strategies of each game.

Equipment

Volleyball, tennis-height net (a volleyball, tennis, or badminton net might be used), court (volleyball, tennis, or badminton)

Procedures

1. Position two teams of three to six players each on either side of the net. Designate one team as the serving team.
2. To begin the game, the right back player on the serving team serves underhand from behind the back line.
3. The ball must bounce once inside the *serving* team's court. Then one of the serving team's front line players must hit the ball over the net.
4. The ball may not touch the net on the service or bounce over the net without assistance by a front player. The server is allowed only one attempt to serve legally.
5. The ball must bounce once on the receiving team's side before the receiving team returns it over the net. Thereafter, it need not bounce between hits if the team needs three hits to return it.

6. Violation of any of the following rules results in a dead ball. In such a situation, either a sideout or a point is awarded depending on whom the violation is against.
    a. The ball may be volleyed or passed, as in volleyball; it may also be stroked, as in tennis, with a closed or open hand. The ball may not be caught, scooped, or lifted.
    b. No more than three players may play the ball on one side of the net. A player may touch the ball twice before it is returned but not twice in succession. If two players contact the ball simultaneously it counts as two contacts for the team.
    c. A ball striking a player at the knee or above and bouncing directly off may be continued in play as though that player had struck it with the hand. The ball may not be kicked or punted.
    d. A player may play the ball when any part of it has crossed the top of the net. However, a player may not reach *over* the net to play a ball, nor may a player's hands follow through over the net.
    e. No player may touch the net or reach over or under the net. Nor may any player cross the center line while the ball is in play.
    f. Net balls, other than serves, may be recovered and played either directly from the net or on the bounce after hitting the net.
    g. A ball that touches any foreign object outside of the court is declared a dead ball.
7. Rotate and score for Volley Tennis in the same way as volleyball.

Variation

Teams play without a net (this is called Bound Ball).

Frisbee Football (Grades 6–12)

Equipment

Frisbee, cones or flags, vests or pinnies

Procedures

1. Divide the class into two teams and position them in scattered formation on a football field. Play four ten-minute quarters.
2. Select one team to throw the Frisbee from midfield at the beginning of the first and third quarters. The other team throws the Frisbee to start the second and fourth quarters.
3. Offensive team members keep the Frisbee in play, throwing it from player to player and advancing it down the field to score a goal.
4. Members of the opposite team try to intercept the Frisbee.

5. The player holding the Frisbee cannot run with it. A two-step stop is allowed when a player catches the Frisbee.
6. When the offensive team is able to catch the Frisbee in the opposite team's end zone, the offense scores six points. If the Frisbee touches the ground in the end zone and is then retrieved by an offensive player, the offense scores three points.
7. Players are not allowed to grab the Frisbee from an opponent or touch one another during the game.
8. Violations entitle the opposite team to take a free throw from the point of the infraction.
9. Each time one team scores points, both teams line up as they did to start the game. The nonscoring team then begins to throw the Frisbee.

Team Handball (Grades 6–12) (Figure 10.23)

Team handball is an exciting and challenging game that combines skills from basketball, soccer, water polo, and hockey.

Equipment

Official handball, volleyball, or small playground ball, vests or pinnies

FIGURE 10.23
Team Handball Court.

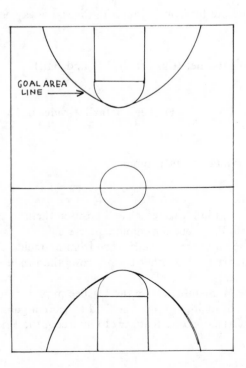

GOAL AREA
LINE →

Procedures

1. Position six players and one goalie from each team on the court. The six court players cover the entire court.
2. Players attempt to advance the ball down the court and score a goal in the opponents' goal area. The team earns one point for a goal.
3. Players may dribble or pass the ball. To score a goal, a player must throw the ball into the opponents' goal area.
4. A player may take three steps before and after dribbling the ball. There is no limit on the number of dribbles any player may take. (However, discourage players from dribbling because passing is more effective.)
5. The following violations result in a free throw from the point of the violation or the edge of the goal area:
   a. Double dribble
   b. Holding the ball longer than three seconds before passing, dribbling, or shooting
   c. Kicking the ball (except the goalie)
   d. Entering the goal area (except the goalie)
6. A penalty throw is awarded from the penalty line (free throw line) when an offensive player inside the goal area line fouled during the act of shooting. During a penalty throw, all players except for the shooter and goalie must remain behind the goal area line. The shooter earns one point for making a penalty throw.

Variation

Allow any number of students on each team.

INDEX